HONORING THE CIRCLE:
ONGOING LEARNING FROM AMERICAN
INDIANS ON POLITICS AND SOCIETY,
VOLUME II

Honoring the Circle:

Ongoing Learning from American Indians on Politics and Society,

Volume II

The Continuing Impact of American Indian Ways in North America and the World in the Nineteenth Century and Beyond

Stephen M. Sachs, Sally Roesch Wagner. Ain Haas, Walter S. Robinson

Waterside Productions

Printed in the United States of America

First Printing, 2020

ISBN-13: 978-1-949001-85-3   print edition
ISBN-13: 978-1-949001-86-0   ebook edition

Honoring the Circle, Volume I
ISBN-13: 978-1-949001-83-9

Honoring the Circle, Volume II
ISBN-13: 978-1-949001-85-3

Honoring the Circle, Volume III
ISBN-13: 978-1-949001-87-7

Honoring the Circle, Volume IV
ISBN-13: 978-1-949001-89-1

Waterside Productions
2055 Oxford Ave.
Cardiff, CA 92007
www.waterside.com

OVERVIEW OF *HONORING THE CIRCLE*

Four Volumes on What the West Has Learned and Still Might Learn from American Indians on Politics and Society

Volume I begins with a prelude, which includes an introduction to *Honoring the Circle* and chapter 1, "Traditional American Indian Politics and Society," a look at how inclusive participatory American Indian societies functioned well. Part I "The Impact of American Indian Tradition on Western Politics and Society," spans over two volumes. It begins in this volume with an introduction and chapters 2 and 3. Chapter 2, "The Impact of American Indians on Politics and Society in the American Colonies and the United States from Contact to 1800," covers the mixture of Indian and European influences on early American settlers, and the Indian influences on major leaders and on the development of American political institutions. Chapter 3, "The Considerable Effect of Contact on Europe," examines the impact of reports of Indians in Europe on all political philosophies.

Volume II continues part I. Chapter 4, "The Continuing Impact of American Indian Ways in North America and the World in the Nineteenth Century and Beyond," covers Native impacts on the development of the American philosophy of pragmatism, the women's movement, the 1960s youth movement, and the environmental movement. The volume closes with a conclusion to part I.

Volume III begins part II, "The Continuing Relevance of American Indian Ways and Values," which discusses learning from

Indians on living well together and with the Earth. It includes an introduction on changes in Western society toward Indigenous ways of seeing and other factors that make Indigenous thinking increasingly relevant for solving major contemporary problems. Chapter 5, "Applying American Indian Principles of Harmony and Balance to Renew the Politics of the Twenty-First Century," and chapter 6, "Returning to Reciprocity: Reconceptualizing Economics and Development," cover politics and economics, including how Indigenous values of inclusive participation and mutual support can provide for well-working societies today, empowering an informed active citizenry with essentially equal political and economic power to participate on an equal basis, with participatory public and private organizations.

Volume IV continues part II. Chapter 7, "Indigenizing the Greening of the World: Applying an Indigenous Approach to Environmental Issues," discusses how holistic Indigenous thinking is necessary for dealing with environmental issues. Chapter 8, "Facilitating the Unfolding of the Circle: Indigenizing Education for the Twenty-First Century," suggests how education at every level can be improved with the Indigenous approach of empowering unique people to learn experientially, as whole people, living in community. The conclusion to *Honoring the Circle* discusses how continuing to integrate Indigenous ideas into our thinking provides a path for living well together and with the planet. It shows how this approach is increasingly at the forefront of political and social discussion.

TABLE OF CONTENTS

PART I (CONTINUED)

THE IMPACT OF AMERICAN INDIAN TRADITION ON WESTERN POLITICS AND SOCIETY

Chapter 4

The Continuing Impact of American Indian Ways in North America and the World in the Nineteenth Century and Beyond

Stephen M. Sachs, Sally Roesch Wagner,
Ain Haas, and Walter S. Robinson

Section 1: Introduction

Stephen M. Sachs

The intertwining of American Indians with the culture of the United States and the ongoing, conscious use of Indian symbols continued after the close of the eighteenth century. Indeed, at least until well into the nineteenth century, a great many US citizens saw their culture as a blend of the Indian and the European, which was now visualized as being "American."[1]

The nineteenth century was a difficult one for Native peoples, suffering dispossession of lands, trails of tears, and a horrendous physical and cultural genocide at the hands of European Americans.[2] Some would say that the cultural impacts on Europeans were another appropriation. There is some truth in that, but what occurred was much more. If the Indianization of arriving colonists, attempted by Indians in the first years of contact, had largely succeeded, it is likely that the ensuing relations and interactions would have been much different. Indeed, at the end of the nineteenth century and the beginning of the twentieth, Indian leaders such as Charles Eastman and later Ella Deloria made a conscious effort to convince European Americans of the virtues of traditional Indigenous American ways; these efforts included Eastman's work of contributing aspects of Indian lore and woodcrafts to the Boy Scouts' and Camp Fire Girls' training and practices.[3]

The interweaving of Indian and European culture in the emerging American identity is immediately visible in the political realm, in the Great Seal of the United States. It was designed at the request of Congress in 1782[4] by Secretary to Congress Charles Thomson, who had been adopted by the Lenape, or Delaware, Nation. Still in use today, the seal depicts an eagle clutching a bunch of arrows, which is a direct reference to the Haudenosaunee, or Iroquois Confederacy, which used this imagery to symbolize their confederacy. Thomson originally proposed a bunch of five or six arrows, as the Haudenosaunee had long been a confederation of five nations and later expanded to six with the addition of the Tuscarora. Congress, however, changed it to thirteen arrows, one for each state.

The eagle was both a European and Indian symbol. With the Europeans having used guns for centuries, the arrow clearly was an Indian symbol. Above the eagle is a cluster of shining fires, depicted as five pointed stars each emanating out light. In referencing a tribe, nation, or other major political entity, many Indians referred to them as "fires"; thus the Lakota people with their seven bands were known as the "Seven Fires," and the colonies, later states, were termed by Indians as the "Thirteen Fires."

From the onset of the discussion about the Great Seal of the United States in 1776, the focus was on blending Indian and European symbols. Thomas Jefferson had suggested that the seal include a "leatherstocking," a European American frontiersman

4

in Indian buckskin garb. The motto of the United States on the seal is in the European Latin. *E Pluribus Unum*, "From Many One," references the joining of the states into a federation, as the Indians had joined together, and had directly suggested the colonies, later states, do as well.

The fusion of American Indian and European identities in the late colonial and early US period also showed itself in the widespread adaption of the symbol of an Indian woman as the "goddess of liberty."[5] She represented the Indian-catalyzed, greatly expanded, Western idea of freedom. The goddess of liberty was an important symbol used by revolutionaries to build support for fighting for independence from England. So important was this symbol after independence that a statue of the Indian goddess was authorized in 1855 and placed upon the pinnacle of the dome of the US Capitol Building, when its expansion was completed in 1863.

The idea of the goddess was an entirely European idea, as Indians worked with "spirits" and had no goddesses. That the symbol itself was a blend of the European and the Indian was an indication of the great degree to which most European Americans saw themselves as both European and Indian.

The emphasis on Indians and the Indian goddess as major parts of American identity was strongest during the American Revolution and in the years immediately afterward when they represented the young nation's independence from England. While remaining important, the position of the goddess and idea of Indianness weakened over time and began to transform. In time, the symbol of the goddess lost its feathers, and its clothing changed to that of a Roman goddess. But while the outer garments became more European, the Indian remained underneath. Many strands of thought with Indian roots continued, at times flowering and bearing new fruit, though their origins were mostly unrecognized until recently.

The transformation of the Indian goddess and the weakening of other Indigenous-related symbols took place over a long period, and for several primary reasons. First, the inclusion of slavery in the Constitution conflicted with the Native-rooted idea of liberty, which also was not applied to women by the early US mainstream. However, until the invention of the cotton gin in 1830, slavery was in a weak economic condition, and many thought it would die a natural death. Many of the founders, including some southern slave owners, considered slavery a "peculiar" institution at the time of the founding. That changed when the cotton gin made slavery more economically viable in the South.

The second, and stronger, reason for the decline of identity with Indians was the coveting of Indian lands by European Americans. This had often been an issue since the beginning of colonization. In the late colonial and early US periods, however, it was not the central question it would become for the United States in the nineteenth century. Fighting some Indians in the War of 1812 was an important event in eroding the country's identification with Native people. The move away from that identity, and Indian symbols, was accelerated by the launching of the removal of Indians from their lands in the 1830s.

There were, of course, regional and individual differences in views about the appropriateness of Indian removal, and the general treatment of Native peoples. Moreover, aspects of the positive view of Indians remained embedded in much of American culture long after identification with Indians had largely fallen away. That it continued could often be seen in the advertising of products said to be of Indian origin. Even as late as the 1950s references to Indians as a selling point could be seen in numerous seed catalogues.[6]

The symbol of the Indian goddess, though diminished with Indian removal, remained an important part of US mythology through much of the nineteenth century. Auguste Bartholdi undertook a tour of the United States in 1871 to Americanize himself so that he could embody the American conception of liberty into the statue of Liberty he was designing. It was to be presented by France to the United States honoring the US centennial, with a duplicate in Le Havre harbor. Bartholdi found the Indian goddess of liberty to still be an important part of American mythology, and the sculptor combined her with the Greek goddess Minerva in his creation of the Statue of Liberty for New York and Le Havre harbors.

As is developed in this chapter, early in the nineteenth century Indian-influenced thinking continued, and, in some instances, significantly expanded. Those lines of thought became more recessive, or continued with less notice, through much of the middle of the century, until they began to bloom again in several areas in the late nineteenth and early twentieth centuries. This occurred particularly in the rise of the women's movement and in a renewal of the American philosophy of pragmatism. They were part of the beginnings of a major change in US culture moving toward Indigenous ways of seeing, a topic that is developed in the introduction to part II of this book. After World War II a major shift in the way Indians were seen by most Americans occurred, which increased their influence even as mainstream cultural change and the nature of the problems the nation and the world confronted created more space for Indigenous approaches.

The post–World War II shift in the position of Indians and the public perception of them had many causes. Among them were increased and more effective Indian activism, a growth in the number of more educated Indians spurred by the GI Bill of Rights and later expanded education opportunities, and the civil rights movement and the war on poverty with their Indian counterparts. Also among those bringers of change, discussed in sections 4 and 5 of this chapter, were the rise of the US counterculture and the growth of the environmental movement.

Reflections of Indian Ways in Nineteenth-Century US Political Writings

Representative of how the political writers of the early nineteenth century made direct references to Indian ways is John C. Calhoun, in his *A Disquisition on Government and Discourse on the Constitution and Government of the United States*.[7] Like many of the statesmen of his day, as Secretary of War Calhoun was regularly involved in dealings with Indians, particularly with the Haudenosaunee. In considering an appropriate system of federalism as a "government of concurrent majority," which was his view of how US federalism should function, he referred to the Haudenosaunee as a well-working practical example. In its "council of union" or federal government, he described how each member:

> possessed a veto on its decisions; so that nothing could be done without the united consent of all. But this, instead of making the Confederacy weak, or impracticable had the opposite effect. It secured harmony in council and action, and within them a great increase of power. The Six Nations became the most powerful Indian tribe within the limits of our country. They carried their conquest and authority far beyond the country they originally occupied. (pp. 72–73)

In *A Disquisition on Government*, while making reference to the governments of the Roman Republic and Poland, Calhoun laid out his principles for a properly functioning government of concurrent majority. He consistently referred to his observations of the Haudenosaunee, as described in chapter 1, in which, like others before him, he saw the Six Nations' council as functioning with a division of powers, as well as with a veto by each of its constituent units, each of which was democratically responsible to its citizens. Thus Calhoun wrote of government in general:

> But government, although intended to protect and preserve society, has itself a strong tendency to disorder and abuse of its powers, as all experience and almost every page of history testify. The cause is to be found in the same constitution of our nature which makes government indispensable. The powers which it is necessary for government to possess, in order to repress violence and preserve order, cannot execute themselves. They must be administered by men in whom, like others, the individual are stronger than

the social feelings. And hence, the powers vested in them to prevent injustice and oppression on the part of others, will, if left unguarded, be by them converted into instruments to oppress the rest of the community. That, by which this is prevented, by whatever name called, is what is meant by constitution, in its most comprehensive sense, when applied to government. (p. 7)

What I propose is far more limited,—to explain on what principles government must be formed, in order to resist, by its own interior structure, or, to use a single term, *organism*,— the tendency to abuse of power. This structure, or organism, is what is meant by constitution, in its strict and more usual sense; and it is this which distinguishes, what are called, constitutional governments from absolute. It is in this strict and more usual sense that I propose to use the term hereafter.

How government, then, must be constructed, in order to counteract, through its organism, this tendency on the part of those who make and execute the laws to oppress those subject to their operation is the next question which claims attention. (pp. 11–12)

.   .   .   .

And as this can only be effected by or through the right of suffrage,—(the right on the part of the ruled to choose their rulers at proper intervals, and to hold them thereby responsible for their conduct,)—the responsibility of the rulers to the ruled, through the right of suffrage, is the indispensable and primary principle in the foundation of a constitutional government. When this right is properly guarded, and the people sufficiently enlightened to understand their own rights and the interests of the community, and duly to appreciate the motives and conduct of those appointed to make and execute the laws, it is all-sufficient to give to those who elect, effective control over those they have elected.

I call the right of suffrage the indispensable and primary principle; for it would be a great and dangerous mistake to suppose, as many do, that it is, of itself, sufficient to form constitutional governments....

The right of suffrage, of itself, can do no more than give complete control to those who elect, over the conduct of those they have elected. In doing this, it accomplishes all it possibly can accomplish. This is its aim,—and when this is attained, its end is fulfilled....

If the whole community had the same interests, so that the interests of each and every portion would be so affected by the action of the government, that the laws which oppressed or impoverished one portion, would necessarily oppress and impoverish all others,—or the reverse,—then the right of suffrage, of itself, would be all-sufficient to counteract the tendency of the government to oppression and abuse of its powers; and, of course, would form, of itself, a perfect constitutional government....

But such is not the case. On the contrary, nothing is more difficult than to equalize the action of the government, in reference to the various and diversified interests of the community; and nothing more easy than to pervert its powers into instruments to aggrandize and enrich one or more interests by oppressing and impoverishing the others; and this too, under the operation of laws, couched in general terms ;—and which, on their face, appear fair and equal.

. . . .

There is, again, but one mode in which this can be effected; and that is, by taking the sense of each interest or portion of the community, which maybe unequally and injuriously affected by the action of the government, separately, through its own majority, or in some other way by which its voice may be fairly expressed; and to require the consent of each interest, either to put or to keep the government in action. This, too, can be accomplished only in one way,—and that is, by such an organism of the government,—and, if necessary for the purpose, of the community also,—as will, by dividing and distributing the powers of government, give to each division or interest, through its appropriate organ, either a concurrent voice in making and executing the laws, or a veto on their execution. It is only by such an organism, that the assent of each can be made necessary to put the government in motion; or the power made effectual to arrest its action, when put in motion;—and it is only by the one or the other that the different interests, orders, classes, or portions, into which the community may be divided, can be protected, and all conflict and struggle between them prevented,—by rendering it impossible to put or to keep it in action, without the concurrent consent of all.

Such an organism as this, combined with the right of suffrage, constitutes, in fact, the elements of constitutional government. The one, by rendering those who make and execute the laws responsible to those on whom they operate, prevents the rulers from oppressing the ruled; and the other, by making it impossible for any one interest or combination of interests or class, or order, or portion of the community, to obtain exclusive control, prevents any one of them from oppressing the other. It is clear, that oppression and abuse of power must come, if at all, from the one or the other quarter. From no other can they come. It follows, that the two, suffrage and proper organism combined, are sufficient to counteract the tendency of government to oppression and abuse of power; and to restrict it to the fulfilment of the great ends for which it is ordained. (pp. 10–18, 24–26)

In governments of the concurrent majority, each portion, in order to advance its own peculiar interests, would have to conciliate all others, by showing a disposition to advance theirs; and, for this purpose, each would select those to represent it, whose wisdom, patriotism, and weight of character, would command the confidence of the others. Under its influence,—and with representatives so well qualified to accomplish the object for which they were selected,—the prevailing desire would be, to promote the common interests of the whole; and, hence, the competition would be, not which should yield the least to promote the common good, but which should yield the most. It is thus, that concession would cease to be considered a sacrifice,—would become a free-will offering on the altar of the country, and lose the name of compromise. And herein is to be found the feature, which distinguishes governments of the concurrent majority so strikingly from those of the numerical. In the latter, each faction, in the struggle to obtain the control of the government, elevates to power the designing, the artful, and unscrupulous, who, in their devotion to party,—instead of aiming at the good of the whole,—aim exclusively at securing the ascendency of party. (p. 69)

Taking the general principles set out in *A Disquisition on Government*, which were influenced by and consistent with the functioning of the Six Nations, Calhoun applied them in his *Discourse on the Constitution and Government of the United States:*

The government of the United States was formed by the Constitution of the United States;—and ours is a democratic, federal republic.

It is democratic, in contradistinction to aristocracy and monarchy. It excludes classes, orders, and all artificial distinctions. To guard against their introduction, the constitution prohibits the granting of any title of nobility by the United States, or by any State.* The whole system is, indeed, democratic throughout. It has for its fundamental principle, the great cardinal maxim, that the people are the source of all power; that the governments of the several States and of the United states were created by them, and for them; that the powers conferred on them are not surrendered, but delegated and, as such, are held in trust, and not absolutely; and can be rightfully exercised only in furtherance of the objects for which they were delegated.

It is federal as well as democratic. *Federal* on the one hand, in contradistinction to *national* and, on the other, to a *confederacy*. In showing this, I shall begin with the former.

It is federal, because it is the government of States united in a political union, in contradistinction to a government of individuals socially united; that is, by what is usually called, a social compact. To express it more concisely, it is federal and not national, because it is the government of a community of States, and not the government of a single State or nation. (pp. 112–13)

Thus the Six Nations example was essential to Calhoun, a southerner supporting southern interests including slavery within the United States, which he strongly supported, as long as the interests of his region were sufficiently protected.

Calhoun was nowhere near alone in finding the Six Nations' government excellent in itself, and an excellent example for the United States and the wider world. Among the many of like mind on that issue was Lewis Henry Morgan—somewhat later in the same century, he so believed in the virtues of Haudenosaunee democracy that he undertook a study of their society (referred to and quoted in chapter 1, on American Indian tradition). In undertaking the study, Morgan was aided on several sections of his ethnography by *Donehogawa* (Ely S. Parker), who was *Adodaroh* (*Tadadaho*) of the league.

Morgan's report of the Six Nations was also important, because as Morgan, an evolutionary anthropologist, says in the beginning of chapter 1 of *Ancient Societies*:

Modern institutions plant their roots in the period of barbarism, into which their germs were transmitted from the previous period of savagery. They have had a lineal descent through the ages, with the streams of the blood, as well as a logical development.

Thus, one can learn much about present institutions by studying their development in earlier stages of society.[8] As Morgan says of the Six Nations:

> The Iroquois were a vigorous and intelligent people, with a brain approaching in volume the Aryan average. Eloquent in oratory, vindictive in war, and indomitable in perseverance, they have gained a place in history. If their military achievements are dreary with the atrocities of savage warfare, they have illustrated some of the highest virtues of mankind in their relations with each other. The confederacy which they organized must be regarded as a remarkable production of wisdom and sagacity. One of its avowed objects was peace; to remove the cause of strife by uniting their tribes under one government, and then extending it by incorporating other tribes of the same name and lineage. They urged the Eries and the Neutral Nation to become members of the confederacy, and for their refusal expelled them from their borders. Such an insight into the highest objects of government is creditable to their intelligence. Their numbers were small, but they counted in their ranks a large number of able men. This proves the high grade of the stock.
>
> From their position and military strength they exercised a marked influence upon the course of events between the English and the French in their competition for supremacy in North America. As the two were nearly equal in power and resources during the first century of colonization, the French may ascribe to the Iroquois, in no small degree the overthrow of their plans of empire in the New World.[9]

What could be learned from the Six Nations, and also from numerous other Indian federations discussed by Morgan in *Ancient Societies*, was extremely important for the United States and the wider world. This was indicated in a letter to Henry R. Schoolcraft, in 1847. Morgan stated that he had established "Orders of the Iroquois," clubs for young men, in order to "teach the materials for our Constitution which we have endeavored to adapt exactly to the original system" through engaging in a "correspondence with educated Indians."[10] He added:

> If we did not believe that the "New Confederacy" [the US federal government] could be made the great repository of Indian Intelligence for the Republic, and thus become an institution of value and usefulness, and if we did not anticipate the cooperation of the cultured and distinguished minds of the Nation, we should certainly despair.

The Example of the Tammany Societies

An example of both the amalgam of Native American and European culture in the emergent American identity and the continued use of Indian symbols is the long history of Tammany societies, first in the colonies and then in the states. Included among these was the New York City political organization Tammany Hall, founded in 1786 and incorporated on May 12, 1789.[11] Tammany (*Tamenund* or *Tamanend*) was a Lenape (Delaware) chief known for his wisdom, who had good relations with William Penn, and became a folk hero among the colonials. During the Revolutionary War, admiring colonists named him Saint Tammany, Patron Saint of America. Numerous Tammany Societies were established among the colonies, many of which flourished well into the nineteenth century, reflecting a considerable popular interest in frontier and Indian life, customs and language.

The Smithsonian's highly regarded *Handbook of Indians North of Mexico* notes the following, concerning the Tammanies:

It appears that the Philadelphia society, which was probably the first bearing the name, and is claimed as the original of the Red Men secret order, was organized May 1, 1772, under the title of Sons of King Tammany, with strongly Loyalist tendency. It is probable that the "Saint Tammany" society was a later organization of Revolutionary sympathizers opposed to the kingly idea. Saint Tammany parish, La., preserves the memory. The practice of organizing American political and military societies on an Indian basis dates back to the French and Indian war, and was especially in favor among the soldiers of the Revolutionary army, most of whom were frontiersmen more or less familiar with Indian life and custom.

The society occasionally at first known as the Columbian Order took an Indian title and formulated for itself a ritual based upon supposedly Indian custom. Thus, the name chosen was that of the traditional Delaware chief; the meeting place was called the "wigwam"; and there were thirteen "tribes" or branches corresponding to the thirteen original states, the New York parent organization being the "Eagle Tribe," New Hampshire the "Otter Tribe," Delaware the "Tiger Tribe," whence the famous "Tammany tiger," and so forth. The principal officer of each tribe was styled the "sachem," and the head of the whole organization was designated the kitchi okeemaw, or grand sachem.[12]

Tammany Hall, or in the early days, the Sons of Saint Tammany or the Columbian Order, was originally a social club, but by the late eighteenth century it had become a political organization associated with the Democratic-Republican Party, later known as the Democratic Party. Until perhaps mid-century, Tammany Hall was a discussion place for new social and political ideas. After the Revolutionary War, Tammany Hall worked to foster democracy, independence, and the federal union, opposing oligarchic power and tendencies. Later in the nineteenth century, Tammany Hall began to assist immigrants, especially the Irish, creating a system of patronage that eventually led to its becoming a corrupt urban political machine. Today the name remains, but little of its original Indian connection does in what is now the New York City Democratic Party.

Exemplifying Tammany Hall and more generally the various nineteenth-century Tammany Societies' appreciation of Indian ways, and most particularly the democratic virtues of Haudenosaunee society, DeWitt Clinton—a Tammany Hall member, former New York assemblyman, mayor, senator, and later governor, member of the Erie Canal Commission, and presidential candidate—presented "A Discourse [on the Six Nations] Delivered Before the New York Historical Society, at their Anniversary Meeting. 6th December, 1811."[13] Clinton spoke of the Six Nations, whom he had recently visited on a journey to western New York, saying, in part:

> We may with equal confidence assert, that morbid must be his sensibility and small must be his capacity for improvement, who does not advance in his wisdom and virtue, from contemplating the state and history of the people who occupied this country before the man of Europe.
>
> As it is therefore not uninteresting, and is entirely suitable to this occasion, I shall present a general geographical, political and historical view of the red men who inhabited this state before us; and this I do the more willingly, from a conviction that no part of America contained a people which will furnish more interesting information and useful instruction—which will display the energies of the human character in a more conspicuous manner, whether in light or in shade-in the exhibition of great virtues and talents, or of great vices and defects. (p. 6)

He also compared the Six Nations to Rome:

> The remaining and much greater part of the state was occupied by the Romans of this Western World, who composed a federal republic. (p. 9)

And spoke of the work of the confederation:

All their proceedings were conducted with great deliberation, and were distinguished for order, decorum and solem-
nity. In eloquence, in dignity, and in all the characteristics
of personal policy, they surpassed an assembly of feudal
barons, and perhaps were not far inferior to the great
Amphyctionic Council of Greece. (p. 15)

The Continuing Impact of Indians on American Thinking

The influence of American Indians on North American thought
and practice has continued in many fields since the opening of the
nineteenth century. The following sections discuss the continuing development of an American philosophy of pragmatism with
strong Native roots and the huge Indigenous encouragement of the
women's movement in the United States and beyond, as well as new
and continuing Indian influences on the countercultural and environmental movements. Meanwhile, the Indian-rooted democratic
and federalist traditions and institutions have lived on, though
with occasional modification. However, memory of that influence
faded in the twentieth century until the work of Grinde, Johansen,
Wagner, Pratt, Lyons, Mohawk, Porter, Shenandoah, Thomas
Barreiro, and others began to revive it.[14]

In addition to the continuing traditions, new learnings from
Native people have been ongoing. Examples include the many
Indians doing environmental work, discussed below, as well as
the environmental movement making references to the Indians as
maintaining balanced relations with all around them, and not taking more of anything than needed. Well-known examples in the
late twentieth century are the public service advertisement showing an Indian in a canoe crying upon seeing polluted waters, the
circulation of what is alleged to be Chief Sea'th'l's ("Seattle" or
"Sealth" are Anglicized) 1854 farewell speech (discussed in the part

II environmental chapter), and the April 1992 environmental gathering in Penn Valley Park, Kansas City, where recycled items were placed in the shape of a huge turtle to represent the many tribes who refer to North America as Turtle Island.[15]

Another new learning from Indians was Erik Erikson's groundbreaking theory in the 1950s on the stages of human child development based on observing Oglala Lakota and Yurok childrearing practices.[16] The gay, lesbian, and transgender movement of today has also gained inspiration from the way people with other than heterosexual gender identifications have found respected roles in traditional Native societies.[17]

Section 2: The Ongoing Indian Aspects of the American Philosophy of Pragmatism[18]

Stephen M. Sachs

A particularly important result of the interaction of Europeans and American Indians in North America has been the rise and evolution of the American philosophy of pragmatism. Pragmatism can generally be described as having the following qualities or emphases: Primary, in agreement with one of the major American Indian values, is the importance of diversity, a valuing of difference, and respect for all people, interests, and views. This is sometimes called the importance of place, respecting that each location in time, space, and way of seeing is different and needs to be respected. From valuing diversity comes the importance of inclusiveness, democracy, and individual rights. But the rights, and the diversity, arise within community. As Native people say, all are related. There are appropriate relations or balances to be maintained between the whole and the parts, and among the parts. This view also sees human understanding as limited, but capable of expanding and in need of learning through experience. Thus, life is experimental, and pragmatism deals with finding what is practical for each within the context of the community, and for the good of the community.

Pragmatism is essentially focused on problem solving, rather than on gaining ultimate knowledge. Since it concerns the needs of limited people to learn through experience for the general as well as the personal good, there is a need for openness of discussion, and continual questioning. Pragmatism is opposed to absolutism and repression, and has often been a vehicle of resistance and liberation.

By 1800, an American philosophy of pragmatism had become well established through the Indianization of important American leaders, including Roger Williams, Benjamin Franklin, Thomas Jefferson, Thomas Paine, and numerous others discussed in chapter 2, and more fully detailed in Scott L. Pratt's *Native Pragmatism*. Moreover, in the course of gaining independence from Great Britain, a widespread American identity developed as being a combination of both the Indian and the European. This continued after 1800, along with the pervasiveness in the United States of Native images, motifs, themes, and ideas. While these receded as the century unfolded, particularly after Indian removal began in the 1830s, they continued as important, though at times recessive, strands of thought in American thinking and consciousness. This provided the ongoing dynamic context for the continuing and developing American philosophy of pragmatism.

Continuing Interchange with Indians

In addition, contact with Indians, and new interchanges between Native and European Americans, has never ceased. A continuing dialogue has remained in progress. A good example early in the nineteenth century is Henry Rowe Schoolcraft and his wife, Jane Johnston Schoolcraft.[19] Henry had been Indian agent to the Chippewa around Sault Ste. Marie. Jane, Bamawawagezhikaquay, was a Chippewa woman who prior to the marriage had traveled widely, studying for a time in Ireland. Together the Schoolcrafts published the journal the *Literary Voyager*, which circulated widely in the northeast in 1826 and 1827. It included Chippewa stories and descriptions of the tribe's customs, contributing to the already significant stock of published Indian stories and reports of their ways, which has continued to expand, most notably since the 1960s.

Indianization, Pragmatism, and Human Rights Activism

Perhaps a more important figure is Lydia Maria Child, who at the age of twelve was sent to live with her sister in Norridgewock, Maine, then a growing European American town, surrounded by small settlements of Eastern Abenaki people.[20] Child had considerable interaction with Native people in the area, and later stated that her move to Norridgewock was transformative. She included numerous Indian stories in her writings, beginning in 1827 in her popular children's magazine, the *Juvenile Miscellany*. Child's early writings, including her novel *Hobomok*, concerned Native-white relations[21] and provided a model that developed into an alternate way of telling stories in the European American tradition. Instead of stating moral principles to guide the reader through the unfolding of the tale, Child focused on what she called "domestic detail." She developed the details and logic of situations as the basis of moral judgments.

Through developing the details of concrete situations, Child often challenged, stretched, reinterpreted, and sometimes overturned mainstream moral principles. Her writings, with their Native emphasis on differences of place, set out to transform European American thinking to accept cultural coexistence as part of a pluralist way of seeing. Consistent with that, she was a strong supporter of American Indian rights, and was also active in promoting the rights of women and the abolition of slavery. Thus, she played a major role in developing a counter literary tradition to the moralist approach, and to writers such as James Fenimore Cooper, who is most well-known for his novel *The Last of the Mohicans* and who wrote of the "vanishing Indian."[22] That Indians are peoples of the past, and not the present, is a mistaken perspective still held by many in the United States today.

Indians Who Influenced Child and Others

The Indian influences on Child included contact with Indian and civil rights leader William Apess.[23] Apess was a Pequot of mixed heritage, who lived from 1798 to 1839. In 1829 he was ordained as a Methodist minister, and while making his rounds in 1833 visited the Mashpee on Cape Cod. There, he helped organize the Mashpee Revolt of 1833–34 to help the tribe regain its civil rights and to stop the stealing of its wood. The incident was favorably reported by the *Boston Advocate*.[24] Apess spoke widely on the rights of peoples of color, including Indians, connecting them to the struggles of European Americans to gain their independence. He spoke in many places in New England and New York, where he moved. He authored five books, and a play that he presented in Boston. Apess was nationally known, and in addition to Child is known to have had an influence upon Thoreau, Herman Melville, William Lloyd Garrison, and Frederick Douglass.[25] While the most famous, and perhaps most successful, Indian spokesperson for Native rights in the Jacksonian period, he was not alone.

Others included Ma-ka-tai-me-she-kia-kiak, known as Black Hawk, who lived from 1767 to 1838. He was a band leader and warrior of the Sauk Nation in what is now the US Midwest. With the aid of a newspaper reporter and an editor, *Autobiography of Ma-Ka-Tai-Me-She-Kia-Kiak, or Black Hawk…* was published in 1833.[26]

A number of Cherokee were widely known in the United States, including Elias Boudinot, born Gallegina Uwati, also known as Buck Watie, who lived from 1802 to 1839.[27] He was an influential Cherokee leader who believed acculturation was important to Cherokee survival. Boudinot was appointed by the Cherokee National Council to be the first editor of the nation's newspaper, *The Cherokee Phoenix*, first published in 1826. He soon expanded the name to *The Cherokee Phoenix and Advocate*, indicting his interest in reaching non-Cherokee as well. While fundraising for a Cherokee Nation academy and printing equipment to publish the paper, in 1826, he spoke at First Presbyterian Church in Philadelphia. He focused on the similarities between Cherokees and whites, and how the Cherokees were adapting elements of European American culture. The speech was well received and greatly helped his fundraising. It was published as a pamphlet, "An Address to the Whites." Other Cherokees who were influential among European Americans of the era included Cherokee principal chief John Ross.

Another prominent Cherokee, George Copway, Kah-Ge-Ga-Gah-Bowh (Gaagigegaabaw in the Fiero orthography), meaning "He Who Stands Forever," was a Mississauga Ojibwe writer, ethnographer, lecturer, Methodist missionary, and advocate of Native North Americans.[28] His life extended from 1818 to 1869. In 1847 he published a memoir about his life as a missionary that made him Canada's first literary celebrity in the United States., where he undertook much of his missionary work. The book enjoyed six printings in the first year of publication and became a national best seller. In 1851, he published *The Traditional History and Characteristic Sketches of The Ojibwe Nation,* the first published history of the Ojibwe in English.

Other European American Writers Influenced by Indians before the Civil War

Another of the European American writers who contributed to the rise of a pluralist alternative literature was Catharine Maria Sedgwick.[29] Sedgwick was born in Stockbridge, Massachusetts, in 1785, an area bordering on Native lands, where she enjoyed extensive interaction with the tribal people. She traveled to the Oneida Nation in New York, where she visited a cousin, the descendant of a woman first abducted, and then adopted, by the tribe. In addition, she read the available histories of the Narragansett and Pequot, as well as Roger Williams's *Key into the Language of America.*[30]

In that volume, Williams discusses his extensive interactions with Native people and illuminates a number of Indian practices that support the vision of a peaceful and diverse American community, compatible with notions of tolerance set forth in Native stories. Sedgwick quotes Williams's *Key* in her novel *Hope Leslie*, published a year following the release of Child's *Hobomok*.[31] *Hope Leslie* has a number of important similarities to Child's *Hobomok*. Among them is that *Hope Leslie* is a story of the unfolding of place, telling of people's experiences in their particular circumstances, rather than a parable asserting moral principles or the progress of humanity. In addition, it concerns a marriage between an Indian and a European American. *Hope Leslie* also includes a strong Native woman, Magawisca, who serves as a bridge between the white and Indigenous worlds.

Both novels put forth stories that undermine the widespread, limited, and often negative European American views of both Indians and women. The various writings of Child and Sedgwick flow with the logic of some of the Algonquian traditions and stories they knew that portrayed women as valued, active participants in their communities—communities that valued difference in gender and ethnicity, and more broadly, among all people and all beings.[32]

Philip Gould asserts that both novels serve as a continuation of the work of the Revolutionary War in establishing republican virtues.[33] Gould finds that Child's and Sedgwick's works, and other fiction of the period, reinterpret the Puritan experience to support the new United States, in part feminizing republican virtue. But these writings also involve an Indianization that began with the first American literature instituted by the Puritans, discussed at the beginning of chapter 2. With Child, Sedgwick, and others, that included an emphasis on place and egalitarian pluralism.

The feminization that Gould sees goes back to first contact, when many observers who made reports circulated in North America and Europe commented about the roles of women in North American Indigenous communities. This involved a balanced reciprocity between men and women. That understanding was reflected early on in the European, and later European American, image of the Indian goddess discussed previously. The noticing by Europeans and European Americans, especially women, of the strong position and activity of Indian women in their societies from first contact began to fuel the rise of the beginnings of a feminist movement. Already in 1800, in the United States and western Europe, many women were expressing their opposition to the legal, social, and educational limits placed upon them.[34]

The thread of Indian influence which included an alternate view of gender relations that had gone from the Americas to Europe, impacting such thinkers as John Locke, returned early in the nineteenth century. In England, in the late eighteenth century the leading spokesperson for women's emancipation was Mary Wollstonecraft,[35] whose most notable book in that vein was *The Vindications: The Rights of Men and the Rights of Woman*.[36] Wollstonecraft built on Locke's empirical philosophy, arguing that women were naturally equal to men intellectually and creatively, but were held back from realizing their capabilities by lack of educational opportunity. Wollstonecraft's views crossed the Atlantic in 1818, with Scottish born Frances Wright, who became a US citizen in 1825.[37] She was a strong supporter of women's rights, including advocating birth control and sexual freedom for women. As an activist in the American Popular Health Movement between 1830 and 1840, Wright advocated for women being involved in health and medicine. She worked for universal equality in education, arguing for free public education for all children over two years of age in state-supported boarding schools.

In line with Native principles and the philosophy of pragmatism, Wright's view of universal equality included all people. She strongly opposed slavery, and founded the Nashoba Commune in Tennessee in 1825 as a utopian community to prepare slaves for emancipation. It functioned for only three years, however. In 1821, Wright published *Views of Society and Manners in America*, which brought her to public attention as a critic of the mainstream social norms and policies of the United States.[38] In that publication and elsewhere, she criticized greed, capitalism, and organized religion. That volume was translated into several languages and was widely read in the United States, Great Britain, and the rest of Europe.

The Interrelation of the Feminist and Abolition Movements

By the 1840s, the ideas of freedom and diversity, greatly contributed to by Indians, had brought about interrelated women and black liberation movements. Opposition to slavery in the Americas by Europeans began with its establishment.[39] During the seventeenth century, English Quakers and Evangelicals condemned slavery as un-Christian. By early in the eighteenth century religious opposition to slavery grew as part of the First Great Awakening in England, and in the British colonies in America in the 1730s and '40s.[40]

At the same time the Indian-influenced idea of freedom among European enlightenment thinkers, first articulated by John Locke, began to be voiced as an argument against slavery.[41] Among the first to state this case was member of the British Parliament, James Edward Oglethorpe, founder of the Province of Georgia. Oglethorpe banned slavery in the colony on humanistic grounds, and argued against it in Parliament. He eventually encouraged his friends Granville Sharp and Hannah More to vigorously work for that cause. Britain banned the importation of African slaves in its colonies in 1807 and abolished slavery in the British Empire in 1833.

In the United States, following the American Revolution, northern states banned slavery by the end of the eighteenth century, beginning with Pennsylvania in 1780, but it remained in practice in the South. By 1787, even many of the southern slave owners among the members of the convention that drafted the US Constitution considered it a peculiar institution without a basis in natural law, but saw it as a temporary necessity in the South. As part of a major compromise, slavery was in fact included in the Constitution, but not mentioned by name.[42] Indeed, some of the major southern political leaders, including Thomas Jefferson and George Washington, eventually freed their slaves.[43] In 1808, the United States criminal-ized the international slave trade, and slavery might well have died out had not the invention of the cotton gin given the institution a new economic viability.[44]

The movement to abolish slavery that began to be a major force in the United States in the late 1820s had clear links to the wom-en's rights movement. A large number of the leading abolitionists were women. William Lloyd Garrison's abolitionist newsletter the *Liberator* commented in 1847, "The Anti-Slavery cause cannot stop to estimate where the greatest indebtedness lies, but whenever the account is made up there can be no doubt that the efforts and sac-rifices of the WOMEN, who helped it, will hold a most honorable and conspicuous position."[45] Among these women were a number who had been directly impacted by Indian thinking. They included Lydia Maria Child, who in 1833 wrote *An Appeal in Favor of that Class of Americans Called Africans.*[46]

Emerson and Thoreau

In the first half of the nineteenth century, two of the period's most influential thinkers, Ralph Waldo Emerson and Henry David Thoreau, grew up and added their own Indigenous-impacted con-tributions to the development of American pragmatism. Both were raised and lived in New England, a region where interchange with Indians was continuing, and thinking influenced by and consistent with Indian worldviews was particularly prevalent.

Emerson was born in 1803 in Boston, then a town of 25,000 people.[47] His father was a respected Boston minister. Following his father's death in 1811, his mother moved the family to Concord. In just a few years, Emerson, who had a college education at Harvard, began teaching. He became a lecturer, and as his fame grew he traveled more widely. Books of his essays began being published in 1841.

Emerson grew up immersed in the especially strongly American Indian–influenced culture of New England. In addition to being impacted by the general milieu, Emerson learned a great deal from the pragmatism of Benjamin Franklin, discussed in chapter 2.[48] As Emerson says in his 1824 letter to his aunt, Mary Moody Emerson:

> Don't you admire (I am not sure you do) his [Franklin's] serene and powerful understanding which was so eminently practical and useful…; which seemed to be a transmigration of the Genius of Socrates-yet more useful, more moral, and more pure, and a living contradiction to the buffoonery that mocked a philosophy in the clouds? …
>
> [Franklin was] a sage who used his pen with a dignity and effect which was new, and had been supposed to belong only to the sword….
>
> One enjoys a higher conception of human worth in measuring the vast influence exercised on men's minds by Franklin's character than even by reading books of past ages…. Many millions have already lived and millions more are now alive who have felt through their whole lives the powerful good effect of both of Franklin's actions and his writings.[49]

Emerson was more closely impacted by Indian thinking through his friendships with several people who often interacted directly with Natives. Particularly important were his close friendship with Thoreau and his interchanges with his brother Charles, an activist against Indian removal. Emerson became involved in this effort, which can be seen in his letter to President Buchanan protesting the removal of the Cherokee to the Indian Territory, which became what is now Oklahoma.[50] Among others with personal Indian experience whom Emerson knew well were Lydia Maria Child and Margaret Fuller, who worked for women's and Indian rights.

Emerson did have some direct contact with Indians. He heard and spoke with a number of Indian leaders who came to Boston to protest the treatment of Indian nations by the US government.[51]

But this contact was limited. Thus, the considerable American Indian influence on Emerson's thinking was mostly indirect.

There were other influences on Emerson's thoughts. These included various European currents of thought in his Massachusetts milieu, and those gained in his education. There was also influence from Hinduism, or Vedantic philosophy, of the Indians of the East.[52] This way of seeing, with its still strong Indigenous roots carried forward in the Vedas, was closer to the American Indian worldview than the European one. Amid the various sources open to him, Emerson developed his own views creatively to launch an "American Transcendentalism,"[53] which Robert Richardson characterizes as follows:

> American Transcendentalism takes its name from Kant's Transcendental Idealism. It can also be thought of as an American Idealism, but neither label satisfactorily suggests the strength of thought or the practical accessibility of the movement that is personified and centered in Emerson. Emersonian Individualism is a protest against social conformity, but not against society. It is a protest on behalf of the autonomous, unalienated human being. There comes a time in everyone's education, he says, when one "arrives at the conclusion that envy is ignorance; that imitation is suicide; that he must make himself for better, for worse, as his portion." Emerson's self-reliant individual is a person who is interested in self-rule—in autarchy not anarchy, a person who acknowledges his equality, and necessary connection with others.[54]

Emerson's approach fits very well with that American Indian view of the autonomous and responsible individual functioning within the web of relationships of a fully democratic society. For Emerson, as for the Indian, it means asserting one's freedom for the general good, and the good of each person. This requires a respectful activism, in which Emerson engaged and encouraged others to do so as well. It found him cooperating in social activism with a number of notable people,[55] some of whom were influenced directly by Indians. These included Lydia Maria Child, and most importantly, Thoreau, who was moved to support John Brown and the emancipation of slaves. Among the others Emerson directly influenced were Margaret Fuller, who worked on Indian rights and later joined in the struggle for Italian independence, and Sophia Peabody, who was engaged in defending Indian rights and education reform. Her reform work especially concerned the movement to establish kindergartens. Emerson's own activism embraced the emancipation of slaves and women, and the defense of the rights of Indians.

A central part of Emerson's worldview was a concern for nature. His 1836 essay "Nature" includes many illustrations of the compatibility of his way of seeing to that of Native Americans. He opens the essay with an Indigenous-like statement of the importance of personal direct experience:

> Our age is retrospective. It builds the sepulchres of the fathers. It writes biographies, histories and critiques. The foregoing generations beheld God and nature face to face. We, through their eyes. Why should we not we also enjoy an original relation to the universe? Why should we not have a poetry and philosophy of insight and not of tradition, and a religion of revelation to us, and not the history of theirs?[56]

> That, as for the Indian, no one can own the land:
> The charming landscape I saw this morning is indubitably made up of some twenty or thirty farms. Miller owns this field, Locke that, and Manning the woodland beyond. But none of them owns the landscape. There is a property in the horizon that no man has but whose eye can integrate all the parts, that is, the poet. That is the best part of these men's farms, yet to this their warranty-deeds give no title.[57]

That life is education through experience, and education
life,

Thus is the unspeakable but intelligible and practicable
meaning of the world conveyed to man. To this one end of
Discipline all parts of Nature conspire.[58]

But, that learning includes intuition, and seeing within,
encompassing what Indians comprehend as vision.

Empirical science is apt to cloud the sight, and by the very
knowledge of functions and processes to bereave the student of the manly contemplation of the whole. The savant
becomes unpoetic. But the best read naturalist who leads
an entire and devout attention to truth, will see that there
remains much to learn of his relation to the world, and
that it is not to be learned by any addition or subtraction
or other comparison of known quantities, but is arrived at
by untaught sallies of the spirit, by a continual self-recovery,
and by entire humility. He will perceive that there are far
more excellent qualities in the student then preciseness
and infallibility; that a guess is often more fruitful than
an indisputable affirmation, and that a dream may let us
deeper into the spirit of nature than a hundred concerted
experiments.[59]

On the importance of each place within the circle of the
whole,

Herein is especially apprehended the unity of Nature —
the unity in variety—which meets us everywhere .... A leaf,
a drop, a crystal, a moment in time, is related to the whole,
and partakes of the perfection of the whole. Each particle
is a microcosm and faithfully renders the likeness of the
world.[60]

And on the need for healing, to return to harmony—or
as the Dine say—beauty,

The reason why the world lacks unity, and lies broken and in heaps, is because man is disunited within himself. He cannot be a naturalist until he satisfies all the demands of the spirit.[61]

Emerson's influence has been wide and long, including playing a major role in the development of the American philosophy of pragmatism with its participatory, socially concerned practical emphasis. That influence began as a mutual influence among friends and collaborators as described below.

Henry David Thoreau

Among Emerson's friends and colleagues who expanded upon his American transcendentalism the most, was Henry David Thoreau (July 12, 1817–May 6, 1862).[62] In writing Thoreau's eulogy upon his death in 1863, Emerson said of him:

No college ever offered him a diploma, or a professor's chair; no academy made him its corresponding secretary, its discoverer, or even its member. Perhaps these learned bodies feared the satire of his presence. Yet so much knowledge of Nature's secret and genius few others possessed, none in a more large and religious synthesis. For not a particle of respect had he to the opinions of any man or body of men, but homage solely to the truth itself; and as he discovered everywhere among doctors some leaning of courtesy, it discredited them. He grew to be revered and admired by his townsmen, who had at first known him only as an oddity. The farmers who employed him as a surveyor soon discovered his rare accuracy and skill, his knowledge of their lands, of trees, of birds, of Indian remains, and the like, which enabled him to tell every farmer more than he knew before of his own farm; so that he began to feel as if Mr. Thoreau had better rights in his land than he. They felt, too, the superiority of the character which addressed all men with a native authority.

Indian relics abound in Concord,—arrow-heads, stone chisels, pestles, and fragments of pottery; and on the river-bank, large heaps of clam-shells and ashes mark spots which the savages frequented. These, and every circumstance touching the Indian, were important in his eyes. His visits to Maine were chiefly for love of the Indian. He had the satisfaction of seeing the manufacture of the bark-canoe, as well as of trying his hand in its management on the rapids. He was inquisitive about the making of the stone arrow-head, and in his last days charged a youth setting out for the Rocky Mountains to find an Indian who could tell him that: "It was well worth a visit to California to learn it." Occasionally, a small party of Penobscot Indians would visit Concord, and pitch their tents for a few weeks in summer on the river-bank. He failed not to make acquaintance with the best of them; though he well knew that asking questions of Indians is like catechizing beavers and rabbits. In his last visit to Maine he had great satisfaction from Joseph Polis, an intelligent Indian of Oldtown, who was his guide for some weeks.

He was equally interested in every natural fact. The depth of his perception found likeness of law throughout Nature, and I know not any genius who so swiftly inferred universal law from the single fact. He was no pedant of a department. His eye was open to beauty, and his ear to music. He found these, not in rare conditions, but wheresoever he went. He thought the best of music was in single strains; and he found poetic suggestion in the humming of the telegraph-wire.[63]

Thoreau was immensely interested in Indians and their relation to the land and to nature. Searching through all Thoreau's known writings, Bradley Dean found 1,074 references to them.[64] Sometimes in his writings Thoreau reflected on finding some Indian artifact:

A curious incident happened some four or six weeks ago which I think it worth the while to record. John and I had been searching for Indian relics, and been successful enough to find two arrowheads and a pestle, when, of a Sunday evening, with our heads full of the past and its remains, we strolled to the mouth of Swamp-bridge brook. As we neared the brow of the hill forming the bank of the river, inspired by my theme, I broke forth into an extravagant eulogy on those savage times, using most violent gesticulations by way of illustration. "There on Nawshawtuct," said I, "was their lodge, the rendezvous of the tribe, and yonder, on Clamshell hill their feasting ground. This was no doubt a favorite haunt; here on this brow was an eligible look-out post. How often have they stood on this very spot, at this very hour, when the sun was sinking behind yonder woods, and gilding with his last rays the waters of the Musketaquid, and pondered the days success and the morrow's prospects, or communed with the spirits of their fathers gone before them, to the land of shades—"Here," I exclaimed, "stood Tahatawan; and there, (to complete the period,) is Tahatawan's arrowhead." We instantly proceeded to sit down on the spot I had pointed to, and I, to carry out the joke, to lay bare an ordinary stone, which my whim had selected, when lo! the first I laid hands on, the grubbing stone that was to be, proved a most perfect arrowhead, as sharp as if just from the hands of the Indian fabricator!!![65]

Sometimes Thoreau referred to Indians in expressing his appreciation of nature:

Nothing is so beautiful as the tree tops. A pine or two with a dash of vapor in the sky—and our elysium is made.—Each tree takes my own attitude sometime. Yonder pine stands like Caesar. I see Cromwell, and Jesus, and George Fox in the wood, with many savages beside. A fallen pine, with its green branches still freshly drooping, lies like Tecumseh with his blanket about him. So the forest is full of attitudes, which give it character.[66]

On occasion Thoreau reports on his interactions with Indians:

The rail-road from Bangor to Oldtown is civilization shooting off in a tangent into the forest.—I had much conversation with an old Indian at the latter place, who sat dreaming upon a scow at the water side-and striking his deer-skin moccasins against the planks-while his arms hung listlessly by his side. He was the most communicative man I had met.——Talked of hunting and fishing-old times and new times. Pointing up the Penobscot he observed—"Two or three miles up the river one beautiful country!" And then as if he would come as far to meet me as I had gone to meet him—he exclaimed—"Ugh" one very hard time!" But he had mistaken his man.[67]

And when hunting in Maine with an Indian guide:

A[nd] now some of Joe's Indian traits come out. He said if you wound 'em me sure get 'em. We all landed at once—[ ] reloaded—Joe threw off his hat—fastened his birch with the painter adjusted his waist band—seized the hatchet—& set out. He told me afterward that Before we landed he had seen a drop of blood on the bank—was 2 or 3 rods distant. He proceeded rapidly up the bank & through the woods with a peculiar elastic—noiseless & stealthy tread—looking to right & left on the ground & stepping in the faint tracks of the wounded moose—now and then pointing in silence to a single drop of blood on the handsome shining leaves of the Clintonia borealis which on every side covered the ground—or to a dry fern stem freshly bruised broken—all the while chewing some leaf or else the spruce gum—I

35

followed watching his motions more than the trail of the moose.[68]

On several occasions Thoreau speaks of his view of Indians. Sometimes this shows his agreement with them on the importance of place:

> Wherever I go I am still on the trail of the Indian.—The light and sandy soils which the first settlers cultivated were the Indian corn fields—and with every fresh ploughing their surface is strewn with the relics of their race—
>
> Arrow heads—spear heads, tomahawks, axes—gouges — pestles—mortars—hoes pipes of soap-stone, ornaments for the neck and breast—and other implements of war and of the chace attract the transient curiosity of the farmer— We have some hundreds which we have ourselves collected.
>
> And one is as surely guided in this search by the locality and nature of the soil as to the berries in autumn— Unlike the modern farmer they selected the light and sandy plains and rising grounds near to ponds and streams of water—— which the squaws could easily cultivate with their stone hoes. And where these fields have been harrowed and rolled for grain in the fall—their surface yields its annual crop arrow heads and other relics as of grain.— And the burnt stones on which their fires were built are seen dispersed by the plow on every hand.
>
> Their memory is in harmony with the russet hue of the fall of the year
>
> Instead of Philip and Paugus on the plains here are Webster & Crockett. Instead of the council house is the legislature.[69]

On occasion, Thoreau speaks of Indians' ways in comparison to those of the European Americans:

The charm of the Indian to me is that he stands free and unconstrained in nature—is her inhabitant—and not her guest—and wears her easily and gracefully. But the civilized man has the habits of the house. His house is a prison in which he finds himself oppressed and confined, not sheltered and protected. He walks as if he sustained the roof—he carries his arms as if the walls would fall in and crush him—and his feet remember the cellar beneath. His muscles are never relaxed— It is rare that he overcomes the house, and learns to sit at home in it—and roof and floor—and walls support themselves—as the sky-and trees—and earth.[70]

Here, Thoreau indicates his convergence of view with Native people on the importance of leaning from experience:

Everyone finds by his own experience that the era in which men cultivate the apple and the amenities of the garden, must be different from that of the forest and hunter's life— Gardening is civil and sociable but it wants the vigor and freedom of the forest and the outlaw. Talk of civilizing the Indian! By his wary independence and aloofness he is admitted to a refinement in his untrimmed mistress, which is like the distant but permanent light of the stars, compared with tapers. There are the innocent pleasures of country life,—but the heroic paths are rugged and retired in another sense, and he who treads them studies his plots and parterres in the stars, he gathers nuts and berries by the way and orchard fruits with such heedlessness as berries.

There is something less noble in gardening even than in savage life. It conciliates—soothes—tames Nature. It breaks the horse and the ox, but the Indian rides the horse wild and chases the Buffalo, and not the less worships them both as his gods.

The gardiner [*sic*] takes plants out of the forest and sets them in his garden, but the true child of nature finds them in his garden already wherever they grow, and does not have to transplant them. If the Indian is somewhat of a stranger in nature the gardener is too much a familiar. There is something vulgar and foul in the latter's closeness to his mistress, something noble and cleanly in the former's distance.

Yet the hunter seems to have a property in the moon which even the farmer has not.

Ah!—the poet knows uses of plants which are not easily reported, though he cultivates no parterre; see how the sun smiles on him while he walks in the gardener's aisles, rather than on the gardner.[71]

The comparison continues:

The constitution of the Ind mind appears to be the very opposite to that of the white man. He is acquainted with a different side of nature. He measures his life by winters not summers— His year is not measured by the sun but consists of a certain number of moons, & his moons are measured not by days but by nights— He has taken hold of the dark side of nature—the white man the bright side.[72]

And in discussing the mark or standard by which a nation is judged to be barbarous or civilized, and the barbarities of civilized states:

The savage is far sighted, his eye, like the Poet's,
   "Doth glance from Heaven to Earth, from
   Earth to Heaven,"
He looks far into futurity, wandering as familiarly through the land of spirits as the *civilized* man through his wood lot or pleasure grounds. His life is practical poetry—a perfect epic; the earth is his hunting ground—he lives suns

and winters—the sun is his time-piece, he journeys to its rising or its setting, to the abode of winter or the land whence the summer comes. He never listens to the thunder but he is reminded of the Great Spirit—it is his voice. To him, the lightening is less terrible than it is sublime—the rainbow less beautiful than it is wonderful—the sun less warm than it is glorious.

The savage dies and is buried, he sleeps with his forefathers, & before many winters his dust returns to dust again, and his body is mingled with the elements. The civilized man can scarce sleep even in his grave. Not even there are the weary at rest, nor do the wicked cease from troubling.[73]

And again he stresses the importance of learning from experience:

The savage may be, and often is, a sage. Our Indian is more of a man than the inhabitant of a city. He lives as a man—he thinks as a man—he dies as a man. The latter, it is true, is more learned; Learning is Art's creature; but it is not essential to the perfect man—it cannot educate.[74]

Thoreau's expressed views, including those on education, are consistent with his actions. He studied at Harvard College from 1833 to 1837, studying classics, philosophy, rhetoric, mathematics, and science. According to legend, he refused to pay five-dollars for his sheepskin master's degree diploma because it had no academic merit as it was given automatically three years after completing the bachelor's degree. He is supposed to have said, "Let every sheep keep its own skin."[75] On returning to his home in Concord he became a member of the faculty of the Concord public school. He resigned after a few weeks, however, because he refused to administer corporal punishment.[76] Thoreau and his brother opened the Concord Academy in 1838, an innovative school with a practical experiential bent, including time in nature and visits to local businesses.

The school provided learning for up to twenty-five boys and girls. In several of its aspects, the Concord Academy was a precursor of John Dewey's progressive education, discussed further in chapter 8. Although the school had sufficient students, Thoreau closed it after the death of his brother in 1842.

Thoreau became a close friend of Emerson, serving as tutor for Emerson's sons while living at the Emerson House from 1841 to 1844. There he also served as gardener and editorial assistant for Emerson. Thoreau, as a philosopher of nature, became involved with Emerson's American transcendentalism. As with Emerson, and in the pragmatic tradition of Emerson's beloved Benjamin Franklin, Thoreau's philosophy was practical and social. His practical aspect showed itself during much of his life in Concord in his working in his family's pencil factory.[77] There, he rediscovered the process of making good pencils with inferior graphite, some of which came from a mine operated by Indians in Sturbridge, Massachusetts. Later, Thoreau transformed the factory into a producer of graphite for the electrotyping process.

The social aspect of Thoreau's pragmatism began to show itself in 1845 with what was to be a two-year experiment in living in a small house in the woods on property owned by Emerson at Walden Pond. In part, Thoreau went there to write. But it also involved much more:

> I went to the woods because I wished to live deliberately, to front only the essential facts of life, and see if I could not learn what it had to teach, and not, when I came to die, discover that I had not lived. I did not wish to live what was not life, living is so dear; nor did I wish to practice resignation, unless it was quite necessary. I wanted to live deep and suck out all the marrow of life, to live so sturdily and Spartan-like as to put to rout all that was not life, to cut a broad swath and shave close, to drive life into a corner, and reduce it to its lowest terms, and, if it proved to be mean, why then to get the whole and genuine meanness of it, and publish its

meanness to the world; or if it were sublime, to know it by experience, and be able to give a true account of it in my next excursion.[78]

But in July of 1846 the local tax collector told Thoreau he had to pay six years of back property taxes. Thoreau refused to do so because he objected to slavery and the Mexican war. As a result he was jailed, but only overnight as someone—likely his aunt—paid the taxes for him, against his will. This experience began his thrust into civil disobedience.[79] In January and February 1848, he delivered lectures on "The Rights and Duties of the Individual in relation to Government," which he revised into the essay "Resistance to Civil Government" (also known as "Civil Disobedience"), published by Elizabeth Peabody in the *Aesthetic Papers* in May 1849.[80] Thoreau opens that essay quite consistently with the more libertarian strand of the Indian-influenced thinking of Jefferson and Locke:

I HEARTILY accept the motto,—"That government is best which governs least;" and I should like to see it acted up to more rapidly and systematically. Carried out, it finally amounts to this, which also I believe, —"That government is best which governs not at all;" and when men are prepared for it, that will be the kind of government which they will have. Government is at best but an expedient; but most governments are usually, and all governments are sometimes, inexpedient. The objections which have been brought against a standing army, and they are many and weighty, and deserve to prevail, may also at last be brought against a standing government. The standing army is only an arm of the standing government. The government itself, which is only the mode which the people have chosen to execute their will, is equally liable to be abused and perverted before the people can act through it. Witness the present Mexican war, the work of comparatively a few individuals using the standing government as their tool; for, in the outset, the people would not have consented to this measure.…

But, to speak practically and as a citizen, unlike those who call themselves no-government men, I ask for, not at once no government, but *at once* a better government. Let every man make known what kind of government would command his respect, and that will be one step toward obtaining it. (p. 1)

Thoreau goes on in line with the Indigenous view of the need for holistic thinking, self-reliance within the community, and community members of moral character. He does this, however, with more of the Western emphasis on the individual than the more equal Native stress between individual and community:

Can there not be a government in which majorities do not virtually decide right and wrong, but conscience?—in which majorities decide only those questions to which the rule of expediency is applicable? Must the citizen ever for a moment, or in the least degree, resign his conscience to the legislator? Why has every man a conscience, then? I think that we should be men first, and subjects afterward. It is not desirable to cultivate a respect for the law, so much as for the right. The only obligation which I have a right to assume, is to do at any time what I think right. It is truly enough said, that a corporation has no conscience; but a corporation of conscientious men is a corporation *with* a conscience.… (p. 1)

Unjust laws exist: shall we be content to obey them, or shall we endeavor to amend them, and obey them until we have succeeded, or shall we transgress them at once? Men generally, under such a government as this, think that they ought to wait until they have persuaded the majority to alter them. They think that, if they should resist, the remedy would be worse than the evil. But it is the fault of the government itself that the remedy *is* worse than the evil. *It* makes it worse. Why is it not more apt to anticipate and provide for reform? Why does it not cherish its wise minority? Why does it cry and resist before it is hurt? Why does it not encourage its citizens to be on the alert to point out its faults, and *do* better than it would have them? Why does it always crucify Christ, and excommunicate Copernicus and Luther, and pronounce Washington and Franklin rebels? (p. 2)

Considering that slavery is Thoreau's most immediate concern, he writes:

If the injustice is part of the necessary friction of the machine of government, let it go, let it go: perchance it will wear smooth,—certainly the machine will wear out. If the injustice has a spring, or a pulley, or a rope, or a crank, exclusively for itself, then perhaps you may consider whether the remedy will not be worse than the evil; but if it is of such a nature that it requires you to be the agent of injustice to another, then, I say, break the law. Let your life be a counter friction to stop the machine. What I have to do is to see, at any rate, that I do not lend myself to the wrong which I condemn.

As for adopting the ways which the State has provided for remedying the evil, I know not of such ways. They take too much time, and a man's life will be gone. I have other affairs to attend to. I came into this world, not chiefly to make this a good place to live in, but to live in it, be it good or bad. A man has not every thing to do, but something; and because he cannot do *every thing*, it is not necessary that he should do *something* wrong. It is not my business to be petitioning the governor or the legislature any more than it is theirs to petition me; and, if they should not hear my petition, what should I do then? But in this case the State has provided no way: its very Constitution is the evil. This may seem to be harsh and stubborn and unconciliatory; but it is to treat with the utmost kindness and consideration the only spirit that can appreciate or deserves it. So is all change for the better, like birth and death which convulse the body.

I do not hesitate to say, that those who call themselves abolitionists should at once effectually withdraw their support, both in person and property, from the government of Massachusetts, and not wait till they constitute a majority of one, before they suffer the right to prevail through them. I think that it is enough if they have God on their side, without waiting for that other one. Moreover, any man more right than his neighbors, constitutes a majority of one already. (p. 2)

Where the Indian sufficiently disapproving of the acts of her/his community could move to another band, or be accompanied by likeminded neighbors to start a new community, Thoreau writes:

Under a government which imprisons any unjustly, the true place for a just man is also a prison. The proper place today, the only place which Massachusetts has provided for her freer and less desponding spirits, is in her prisons, to be put out and locked out of the State by her own act, as they have already put themselves out by their principles. It is there that the fugitive slave, and the Mexican prisoner on parole, and the Indian come to plead the wrongs of his race, should find them; on that separate, but more free and honorable ground, where the State places those who are not *with* her but *against* her,—the only house in a slave-state in which a free man can abide with honor. If any think that their influence would be lost there, and their voices no longer afflict the ear of the State, that they would not be as an enemy within its walls, they do not know by how much truth is stronger than error, nor how much more eloquently and effectively he can combat injustice who has experienced a little in his own person. Cast your whole vote, not a strip of paper merely, but your whole influence. A minority is powerless while it conforms to the majority; it is not even a minority then; but it is irresistible when it clogs by its whole weight. (p. 2)

Here, we have the beginning of a far-spreading philosophy of civil disobedience, which ultimately spawned the worldwide non-violence movement. Among many others who were influenced by Thoreau, Mohandas Gandhi read "Civil Disobedience" in South Africa in 1906.[81] He was then fighting the "Black Act," which required Asians to register with the government and to be finger-printed. In refusing to register, Gandhi quoted Thoreau concerning his refusal to pay taxes. Martin Luther King Jr., who learned from Gandhi and went to India on a "pilgrimage to nonviolence," stated in his autobiography that his introduction to the idea of nonviolent resistance was in reading Thoreau's essay "On Civil Disobedience" while in college in 1944.[82] Thus the whole nonviolent resistance movement has a major root in Thoreau's work, from a ground fertilized by both American Indian and European traditions.

Thoreau's social concerns also included a major emphasis on respecting the rights of all people. This included opposing unjust war. This was indicated by his opposition to the Mexican American War, but Thoreau did not go so far as to oppose all violent actions. This is demonstrated, in the course of his opposition to slavery, by his support of John Brown, including Brown's raid on the US arsenal at Harper's Ferry:

Prominent and influential editors, accustomed to deal with politicians, men of an infinitely lower grade, say, in their ignorance, that he acted "on the principle of revenge." They do not know the man. They must enlarge themselves to conceive of him. I have no doubt that the time will come when they will begin to see him as he was. They have got to conceive of a man of faith and of religious principle, and not a politician or an Indian; of a man who did not wait till he was personally interfered with or thwarted in some harmless business before he gave his life to the cause of the oppressed....[83]

I know that the mass of my countrymen think that the only righteous use that can be made of Sharps rifles and revolvers is to fight duels with them, when we are insulted by other nations, or to hunt Indians, or shoot fugitive slaves with them, or the like. I think that for once the Sharps rifles and the revolvers were employed in a righteous cause. The tools were in the hands of one who could use them.[84]

Thoreau, always concerned about nature, as was Emerson, became increasingly immersed with the natural world in his later years as is reflected in his writings, including his 1862 works *Autumnal Tints* (on the colors of leaves in the fall) and *Wild Apples*. In his essay "Walking" he made the often-quoted statement, "In wildness is the preservation of the world."[85]

Both Thoreau and Emerson were widely read in the United States and beyond, and were quite influential. This was particularly true in the development of the environmental movement, beginning in the 1960s, which is discussed below. Together, the two Concord residents, each in his own unique and creative way, continued the Indian blended with European character of America, assisting the further development of American pragmatism later in the nineteenth and into the twentieth century.

Later Nineteenth-Century Activist Intertwinings of Pragmatism

As the nineteenth century continued to unfold past the Civil War and Reconstruction, the intertwining of American Indian–influenced African American and women's emancipation efforts continued, with new Indian inputs, all of which challenged mainstream American thinking. A number of women were at the center of this ongoing development. One of their primary concerns was expanding the concept of place, including home, set forth by Lydia Maria Child.

In 1846, Catharine Beecher published *Treatise on Domestic Economy*.[86] The book expanded Child's *Frugal Housewife* into a domestic science by applying the method of experimental science to show how the home could be a better place for the health and well-being of the entire family. In 1869 Beecher collaborated with her sister Harriet Beecher Stowe to broaden *Treatise* into *The American Woman's Home*,[87] aimed at undermining the hierarchical relationship between men and women. It achieved this, however, by setting out strict roles for men and women based on Christian values. This undercut the diversity expressed by Child, and left an ambiguity between women's empowerment and subservience.

By the 1890s, a new generation of women writers began again to use the logic of home for social change. Among them was Louisa May Alcott.[88] Alcott was born in Germantown, then outside of Philadelphia, in 1832, to educator and transcendentalist Amos Bronson Alcott and social worker Abby May. The family moved in 1834 to Boston, where Amos Alcott founded an experimental school and joined the Transcendental Club with Emerson and Thoreau.

Beginning in 1840, the Alcotts lived in Concord, Massachusetts, except for a short time at the Utopian Fruitlands community in 1843–44. Louisa May Alcott was educated by her father, along with family friends, Emerson, Thoreau, Margaret Fuller, and Nathaniel Hawthorne. As a member of a low-income family, Alcott began work at an early age as a seamstress, teacher, domestic worker, and writer. She read, with admiration, the Seneca Falls Convention on women's rights "Declaration of Sentiments," and was actively part of the antislavery movement with her family, including housing an escaped slave in 1847. The family home became a station on the underground railroad. In 1850, she became the first woman to vote in Concord, in a school board election.

Alcott first gained literary success with *Hospital Sketches*, a critique of the mismanagement of hospitals and the uncaring attitude of some doctors, based on her service as a nurse during the Civil War at Union Hospital at Georgetown, in Washington, DC, in 1862–63.[89] She was an active abolitionist and a feminist. In a number of her writings, Alcott's narratives provide:

> a new ground for the logic of home and a renewed interest in devising a means for women to conceptualize their own circumstances in the context of a particular place. Narratives in this way could provide both a detailed description of a situation and the relations that make it up and provide resources for carrying the relations into a wider situation.[90]

In her novel *Work: A Story of Experience*,[91] for example, Alcott presents a woman striving successfully for a home place in the face of poverty, male domination, exclusion, and civil war. The central character prevails by forming alliances with other women of different racial, ethnic, and class backgrounds.

Another prominent woman in the American pragmatist tradition of the late nineteenth century was Charlotte Perkins Gilman, a sociologist; feminist; writer of nonfiction, poetry, and short stories; and lecturer for social change.[92]

Born in 1860 in Hartford, Connecticut, Gilman was a great niece of Catharine Beecher, with whom she often spent time in her younger years. Much of her youth was spent in Providence, Rhode Island. Gilman followed her great aunt's method of applying experimental science to the problems of human growth and development. In her most important writing, *Women and Economics*,[93] Gilman takes the perspective that human beings can only be understood in terms of their interactions with their environments. In a feminist reconceptualization of Darwin's theory of evolution, she held that men and women, as organisms in particular environments, developed unique modes of interacting following from distinct physiologies and differences in opportunities and expectations. In this she agreed with Child that growth is the standard according to which interaction can be evaluated, and that the framework for women's independence is in the logic of home and the demands of growth. Consistent with the balanced reciprocity of American Indian gender relations, Gilman wrote:

> Granting squarely that it is the business of women to make the home life of the world true, healthful and beautiful, the economically dependent woman does not do this, and never can. The economically independent woman can and will. As the family is by no means identical with marriage, so is the home by no means identical with either.[94]

Diverging from the view of her great-aunt, Gilman asserted that home and society must be seen as continuous because women were stifled and made subservient to the extent that home and society became separate. Where Child and Alcott saw the relations of home as providing the means for social transformation, Gilman, in the developing conditions of the end of the nineteenth century, understood that social transformation could make homes the locus of concrete interactions, places of growth.

Addams and Hull House

Another important contributor to the development of American pragmatism was Jane Addams, born in 1860 in Cedarville, Illinois.[95] Addams cofounded Hull House with Ellen Gates Starr in 1889, in a poor immigrant neighborhood in Chicago. It was the first settlement house in the United States. Her work there caused Addams to be known as the "mother" of social work. An activist and reformer, social worker, sociologist, public philosopher, and author, she was an early leader in the settlement house movement. Addams, who lived until 1935, was also a leader in the movements for women's suffrage and world peace.

Addams built on the logic of home of Child, Alcott, and a number of writers in the abolitionist movement, turning it into a social ethic. She expresses this clearly in *Democracy and Social Ethics,* published in 1902, applying the logic of home, where problems can only be understood in the context of their circumstances, and solutions can only be created within the existing situation.[96] Early on, she makes clear the pragmatist importance of diversity and experience:

> We are learning that a standard of social ethics is not attained by traveling a sequestered byway, but by mixing on the thronged and common road where all must turn out for one another, and at least see the size of one another's burdens. To follow the path of social morality results perforce in the temper if not the practice of democratic spirit, for it implies that diversified human experience and resultant sympathy are the foundation and guarantee of Democracy. (pp. 6–7)

Addams also makes clear that acting properly is not just about right principles, but requires acting according to the specifics of developing situations:

> We slowly learn that life consists of processes as well as results, and that failure may come quite as easily from ignoring the adequacy of one's method as from selfish or ignoble aims. (p. 6)
>
> We do not believe that genuine experience can lead us astray any more than scientific data can.
>
> We realize, too, that social perspective and sanity of judgement come only from contact with social experience; that such contact is the surest corrective of opinions concerning the social order, and concerning efforts, however humble, for its improvement. Indeed, it is a consciousness of the illuminating and dynamic value of this wider and more thorough human experience which explains in no small degree that new curiosity regarding human life which has more of a moral basis than an intellectual one. (pp. 7–8)

We have learned as common knowledge that much of the insensibility and hardness of the world is due to the lack of imagination which prevents a realization of the experience of other people. Already there is a conviction that we are under a moral obligation in choosing our experiences, since the result of those experiences must ultimately determine our understanding of life. We know intuitively that if we grow contemptuous of our fellows, and consciously limit our intercourse to certain kinds of people whom we have previously decided to respect, we not only tremendously circumscribe our range of life, but limit the scope of our ethics. (pp. 9–10)

In concluding her introduction to a series of studies, Addams commented:

of various types of groups who are being impelled by the newer conception of Democracy to an acceptance of social obligations involving a new line of conduct. No attempt is made to reach a conclusion, nor to offer advice beyond the assumption that the cure for the ills of Democracy is more Democracy. (pp. 10–11)

Addams believed that the solutions to the problems of the disadvantaged, whether they were poor, or discriminated-against people, disfavored ethnic or racial groups, or women, could not be externally imposed. What was needed instead was to restructure these people's circumstances, starting with the resources in the places where they were located. Those resources encompassed the material conditions at hand, the experiences, histories, and locations of those concerned and the locations involved, the interests of those involved, and the external forces that frequently made difficult, or prevented, interactions which led to growth. The founding of Hull House was an effort to facilitate the restructuring of the circumstances and resources of the low-income immigrant community of which it was a center, and to provide a space in which the participants could interact progressively.

Her approach, and the operation of Hull House, was very much in keeping with American Indian traditions of participatory inclusiveness, mutual support, and adaptation to changing circumstance through experience. It functioned as an experimental center making progress with successes, while learning from both failure and success. A reflection on its functioning is presented in Addams's *Twenty Years at Hull House*.[97]

But Hull House also had wider functions. These included it serving as a laboratory and model for the settlement house movement, and for its pragmatic approach to dealing with social problems. At times it also served as a meeting place for activist interaction and cross fertilization. During the first wave of "Pan-Indian" activism in the late nineteenth and early twentieth centuries, Hull House brought together leading American Indian women, including Susan LaFlesche and Gertrude Bonin, with African American leaders including W. E. B. Du Bois, and European American philosophers, among them John Dewey, George Herbert Mead, and Josiah Royce.[98]

Dewey met Addams and stayed at Hull House in 1892 while visiting the University of Chicago. While serving as a faculty member at the university from 1894 to 1904, he headed the Philosophy Department and initiated the University of Chicago Laboratory School. Dewey wrote to Addams about his stay at Hull House:

> I cannot tell you how much good I got from my stay at Hull House. My indebtedness to you for giving me insight into matters there is great. While I did not see much of any particular thing I think that I got a very good idea of the general spirit and method. Every day I stayed there added to my conviction that you had taken the right way.[99]

The African American Connection

There was an African American connection to American Indian–influenced American pragmatism, which also linked to Hull House. This built upon the preceding ties of the abolition movement to the Indian-influenced women's emancipation movement, and efforts to protect Native American rights. Some of these were in the similarity of indigenous African ways of seeing and American Indian world-views. Others came from extensive interaction between blacks and Indians in the thirteen colonies, and then, in the United States, including a fair amount of intermarriage.[100] It is notable that Crispus Attucks, the first American killed by British troops in what became the American Revolution, was African American and Indian. Some Indian tribes in the South, including the Cherokee and Seminole, engaged in Negro slavery, and when their slaves were freed at the end of the Civil War, the former slaves became tribal members.[101]

Quite a few African American leaders and writers, beginning in the nineteenth century, had pragmatist strands in their thinking. W. E. B. Du Bois, for example, studied with pragmatist philosophers William James and Josiah Royce (discussed below) at Harvard and developed a conception of self and community similar to theirs. Du Bois's adherence to the importance of place, diversity, and experience is evident in his discussion of race, which he understood not to be based upon biology or lineage alone. In an address "On the Conservation of Race," he stated that race involved:

> A vast family of human beings, generally of common blood and language, always of common tradition, history or impulse, who are both voluntarily and involuntarily striving together for the accomplishment of certain more or less vividly conceived ideals of life.[102]

Thus "race" is primarily cultural, based on common experience and interest or bonding. Such a race can participate in and contribute to a larger common community on an equal basis, when it is not blocked from doing so. The "Negro Race" fits this definition. For Du Bois, concepts of "whiteness" that involve racial white superiority and discrimination against other races are not legitimate because they ran counter to the principles of diversity and mutual respect that underlie this view.

When it came to approaching social problems, including the pressing ones concerning African Americans, Du Bois's work at Harvard with James and historian Albert Bushnell Hart agreed with Addams's approach at Hull House. They believed that major social problems could only be solved in place on the basis of the carefully collected and understood facts from which alternative solutions could be developed and carried out with ongoing corrections to changing circumstances.[103]

As Pratt in *Native Pragmatism* and McKenna and Pratt in *American Philosophy: From Wounded Knee to the Present* have shown, numerous African American activists and thinkers have, to different extents and in different ways, proceeded within the Native-consistent, American pragmatist tradition.[104] For example, civil rights movement leader Martin Luther King Jr. and philosopher Alain LeRoy Locke were influenced by pragmatists James and Peirce (discussed below), as well as more recent pragmatist thinkers.

Cornell West, noting that all approaches can be properly or improperly applied, said of American pragmatist philosophy:

> At its worst, it became a mere ideological cloak for corporate liberalism and managerial social engineering which served the interests of American corporate capital.... [At its best] it survived as a form of cultural critique and social reform at the service of expanding the scope of democratic process and broadening the arena of individual self-development here and abroad.[105]

According to McKenna and Pratt, West found pragmatism "a questioning open ended, antifoundationalist philosophy that is committed to enquiry, democracy and amelioration."[106] In addition to using its methods for his own critiques and proposals for improvement, in *The American Evasion of Philosophy: A Genealogy of Pragmatism*, West examines the unfolding of pragmatism from Emerson to Rorty, concluding with his own "prophetic pragmatism."[107] For West, prophetic pragmatism is "a rich and revisable tradition that serves as the occasion for cultural criticism and political engagement."[108]

James, Peirce, Dewey, et al.: Toward a Contemporary American Pragmatism

By the late nineteenth and early twentieth century the strands of Indigenous American thought among European Americans, going back to first contact, regularly added to by continuing Indian inputs, and reinforced by similar other strands and independent thinking, was developing into a classical American pragmatism led by William James, Charles Sanders Peirce, and John Dewey, among others.[109] While each of these major thinkers had their own approach and emphasis, they were generally in agreement about the nature of pragmatist philosophy. For all of them, in an uncertain existence in which human knowledge and decision-making must always be imperfect, philosophy was concerned with guiding action in communities of diverse individuals on the basis of unfolding experience, rather than attempting to find ultimate principles. As Dewey stated:

> The distinctive office, problems and subject matter of philosophy grow out of stresses and strains in the community life in which a given form of philosophy arises, and that, accordingly, its specific problems vary with the changes in human life that are always going on and that at times constitute a crisis and a turning point in human history.[110]
>
> In other words, whatever else philosophies are or are not, they are at least significant cultural phenomena and

demand treatment from that point of view.... [They are] a
critique of basic and widely held beliefs.[111]

For James, Peirce, and Dewey, the philosophy of pragmatism
was built on four conceptions.[112] The first conception was interaction. Peirce stated this required one to:

consider what effects which might conceivably have practical bearings, we conceive the object of our conception to
have. Then our conception of these effects is the whole of
our conception of the object.[113]

James went a step further in conceiving interaction as having
a practical, or "cash," value so that one can comparatively evaluate
alternative choices, such that one can see "what definite difference
it will make to you and me."[114] Philosophy is practical for James,
because it guides one's choices of actions in a world in which each
person is an actor in a set of reciprocal relations.

Dewey agrees, noting that life is engagement in interdependent
interaction:

The processes of living are enacted by the environment as
truly as by the organism, for they are an integration.[115]

The second conception of classical pragmatism was pluralism.
While interaction involves the connection or unity of things, it also
implies their differences, which arise from differences in experience, both individual and collective: personal and cultural. In this
connection, James observes:

If our intellect had been as much interested in disjunc-
tive as in conjunctive relations, philosophy would have
equally successfully celebrated the world's disunion.
Neither is more primordial or essential or excellent than
the other.[116]

One needs to focus on one or the other depending on the circumstances. Pluralism arises from interaction. Each person and culture obtains knowledge from different, though in some way related, experiences. Each person's and culture's knowledge is incomplete, and can be expanded from the views and knowledge of the other.

Peirce was less radical than James in considering pluralism at the theoretical level, but he was much in agreement with James regarding its importance in practice. In his view, the universe began from one mind, but for human beings every day, variety was:

> beyond comparison the most obtrusive stuff of the universe....[117]
>
> What we call matter is not completely dead, but is merely mind hide-bound with habits. It still retains the element of diversification; and in that diversification, there is life.[118]

Dewey took an effectively similar, but more concrete, view of pluralism:

> That knowledge has many different meanings follows from the operational definition of conceptions. There are as many conceptions of knowledge as there are distinctive operations by which problematic situations are resolved.[119]
>
> If we see that knowing is not the act of an outside spectator but of a participant inside the natural social scene, then the true object of knowledge resides in the consequences of directed action.... For on this basis there will be as many kinds of known objects as there are kinds of effectively conducted operations of enquiry which result in the consequences intended.[120]

In other words, because each person, out of experience, interacts differently with the world to create new experience and thus new ways of seeing, so that there are necessarily a wide variety of ways of knowing and perceiving.

This led to the third conception, community, which, especially for Dewey, required equalitarian interchange of views and dialoguing in an appropriate process of democracy to properly make decisions collectively. Peirce understood individuals to be members of communities. He states:

> What anything really is, is what it may finally come to be known in the ideal state of complete information, so that reality depends on the ultimate decision of the community....
>
> The existence of thought now depends upon what is to be hereafter; so that it has only a potential existence, dependent on the future thought of the community.[121]

James sees human identity inseparable from, and partly commensurate with, community:

> A man's social self is the recognition he gets from his mates. Properly speaking, a man has as many social selves as there are individuals who recognize him and carry an image of him in their minds.... But as the individuals who carry the images fall naturally into classes, we may practically say he has as many social selves as there are distinct groups of persons about whose opinion he cares.[122]

Dewey differs from Peirce, as he does not see anything ultimate or deterministic about thought in terms of community, but rather that conceptions of truth are dependent upon the diversity of cultures and the problems that frame inquiry. Further, it is community which gave rise to language, which provided the basis for enquiry, along with common interests in a shared environment. What was necessary for common language and what arose from it, for Dewey, was the human ability "to take the standpoint of other individuals and to see and enquire from a standpoint that is not strictly personal but is common to them as participants or parties in a conjoint undertaking."[123] For Dewey, this led to a concern for the views of others that extended beyond mere tolerance, to "hospitality": an "open-mindedness" to respect the views of others.

But open-mindedness is not emptiness. It does not lead to a value-free relativism because each participating person maintains his/her own values out of their own ongoing experience, which includes the discussion or interaction.[124] What Dewey saw as necessary to develop, usually arising within a community of interest, is an open-mindedness that is "an attitude of mind which actively welcomes suggestions and relevant information from all sides."[125]

What further prevented classical pragmatism from falling into a value-free relativism was the fourth conception: growth, which serves as a standard for, and a limit upon, community. Proper interaction and deliberation lead to increased knowledge and some practical advance, at a minimum, in terms of the situation or problem under deliberation. It arises in the synergy of sufficiently honest dialogue where the parties are concerned that their individual interests are advanced in realizing a common interest, which is the basis of community. Peirce found this conception of growth being the key to realizing the first three conceptions in his reading of Aristotle.[126]

In this view, growth arises from the conjunction of potential and action, matter and form. Peirce saw this as the interaction of the "female function"—or the seed, and the "male function"— which "exercises a hunch" as a "principle of unrest."[127] Out of the interaction of the two functions arises a third, which is not implicit in either of them, or in the two together prior to interaction. It is an impact that provides the direction and purpose to the particular union to overcome the inertia of habit and the vagaries of chance. This third function Peirce called "creative love."[128] He makes the connection between growth and love explicit in commenting on the Apostle John's proclamation that God is love:

Everyone can see that the statement of St. John is the formula of an evolutionary philosophy, which teaches that growth comes only from love...from the ardent impulse to fulfil another's highest impulse.[129]

James's view on growth was similar to that of Peirce. In *The Varieties of Religious Experience* James states that what is common in religions consists of two parts:

an uneasiness; and...its solution. The uneasiness, reduced to its simplest terms, is a sense that there is something wrong about us as we naturally stand. The solution is a sense that we are saved from the wrongness by making proper connection with the higher powers.

[A person] becomes conscious that this higher part is coterminous and continuous with a more of the same quality, which is operative in the universe outside of him, and which he can keep in working touch with.[130]

For James, growth was both a standard and way of understanding human experience. The standard of growth was the standard of maximizing possibilities and encouraging further growth. In understanding experience, he posits:

Our Acts, our turning-places, where we seem to ourselves to make ourselves and grow, are the parts of the world to which we are closest, the parts of which our knowledge is the most intimate and complete. Why should we not take them at face-value?[131]

For Dewey, there is no separation between organisms, including individuals and communities of people, and their environment, and by its nature an organism is engaged in a growth process. "The reality is the growth process itself."[132] Meaning that growth is an indeterminate process, influenced by the history of the organism and of its environment. For human beings who are conscious, growth is normative. In educational terms, for one in the role of the teacher, both the external teacher and the internal reflective self, it means facilitating the learning experience prior to and during evaluating the experience as, and after, it occurs. According to Dewey, the normative consideration includes:

> from the standpoint of growth as education and education as growth, the question is whether growth in this direction promotes or retards growth in general. Does this form of growth create conditions for further growth, or does it set up conditions that shut off the person who has grown in this particular direction from the occasions, stimuli and opportunity for continuing growth in new directions?[133]

For example, does one who steals learn from that experience to be a more clever thief, or does the person learn that stealing is destructive and that it is personally and socially better to employ his or her talents in a socially constructive and personally rewarding direction? Growth in some direction will always occur as long as an organism is alive. Movement in a direction that is healthy is to be chosen or encouraged, and that which is pathological is to be avoided or discouraged. Limited human beings will at times have difficulty determining which is which. The best guide is what experience indicates will be the results of a choice, and having made a choice, to learn, and hence grow from the results while recognizing the need for continuing reevaluation, as sometimes one learns the wrong lessons.

For Dewey:

> Freedom, in its practical and moral sense … is connected with possibility of growth.[134]
>
> In the degree in which we become aware of possibilities of development and actively concerned to keep the avenues of growth open, in the degree in which we fight against induration and fixity, and thereby realize the possibilities of recreation of ourselves, we are actually free.[135]

Ultimately, such actual freedom requires a democratic community. This allows one to learn and grow through the process of participating. The democratic ideal for Dewey was a community that affirmed the value of individual growth, and realized community growth by providing opportunities for individual growth and through the synergy of the interaction of its diverse members. In this, Peirce, James, and Addams, among many others in the classical pragmatist tradition, concur—despite differences of emphasis, or variation in the details of their explanation.

William James, Pragmatist from Experience

William James, often called the father of American psychology, was born in New York City in 1842 to a well-to-do family.[136] He was educated eclectically at home, and in schools in the United States and Europe. James had broad interests, including the arts. At first, he apprenticed with painter William Morris Hunt. But he soon decided to focus upon science, entering Harvard Medical School in 1864. On graduating from medical school in 1869, he fell into a depressed state for some time. This experience may well have influenced his decision to study psychology.

As an MD, James spent at least fourteen years working to develop a natural science of human psychology. He began attempting to discover laws of functional covariation linking mental states and brain states. Very soon, however, he discovered that proceeding in terms of nineteenth-century science that conceived of the universe as a machine and of a duality between mind and body was unworkable. He quickly found that it was impossible to identify mental states in isolation. He also found that there was no mind-body separation. Mental states were always directly connected to what they were about and to the whole experienced context that gave the subject of the experience its meaning, which was the initiator of the mental state. This led him to think holistically with a major focus upon experience.

James's shift in perspective to become a leader in the development of Native American–influenced classical pragmatism did not occur in a vacuum.[137] His father, Henry James Sr., was a well-known Swedenborgian theologian who interacted with some of the intellectual and literary elites of the time. And James had read Emerson, among others, so that there was a clear chain of thinking and perceiving extending from American Indian influences through Franklin and others to which James's experience could connect. This provided an aid to solidifying James's understanding of his experience. James came to see that people are not merely in the world; they are of it. The individual and his or her environment are in an ongoing dialogue, influencing each other. The individual experiences the world in which they participate through the lens of past and ongoing experience.

For James, experience was not merely concrete, as evidenced by his joining the Theosophical Society in 1882; it focused too upon mystical and experiential Eastern religion, as evidenced in James's writing The Varieties of Religious Experience: A Study in Human Nature in 1902. But if James was in any sense a mystic, he was a practical one. He believed in taking from various theories, including spiritual ones, whatever made good sense, and that then could be proven by experience and analysis.[138]

Thus, in writing The Principles of Psychology, published in 1890, after setting out "psychological preliminaries" in the scientific mode of the day as a detached observer, he relies heavily on his own experience in developing a carefully analyzed psychology. It is a psychology in which any event is perceived within the whole of the context of the perceiver, who perceives through the lens of past experience. Following the principles of pragmatism outlined above, while each person and cultural group has their own individual experience, which needs to be recognized in the practice of individual and social psychology, the fact that all are connected and interacting within the same world, combined with limitations on the varieties of human minds and of human experiences, means that there are also general classifications and principles for a human psychology.

One of the limits that James, other pragmatists, and American Indians recognized is the limitation in human knowledge and understanding. Thus, theory can never be absolute. To be meaningful it must be limited to the context from which it arises and to which it applies. Attributing his thinking on this point to Peirce, James writes:

> To attain perfect clearness in our thought of an object…we need only consider what effects of a conceivable practical kind the object many involve…. Our conception of these effects then, is for us the whole of our conception of the object, so far as that conception has positive significance at all.[139]

Consistent with the four conceptions of classical pragmatism, and Indigenous understanding, the limits in human perception and thought also led James to conclude there was a need for dialogue and democracy:

> Neither the whole of the truth nor the whole of good is revealed to any single observer, although each observer gains a partial superiority of insight from the peculiar position in which he stands.[140]

The Pragmatic Phenomenology of
Charles Sanders Peirce

Charles Sanders Peirce was born in 1839 in Cambridge, Massachusetts, where his father was a respected professor of astronomy and mathematics at Harvard University and a cofounder of the American Academy of Sciences.[141] One important influence in his early life was reading his older brother's copy of Richard Whately's *Elements of Logic*. Peirce had very broad interests and was extremely creative and innovative. He is often considered to be "the father of pragmatism," and also of semiotics: the study of meaning, relating to signs and language. Peirce expanded his focus from work concerning logic to mathematics, chemistry, philosophy, and language. He undertook practical technical work with the United States Coast Survey, and for a few years taught at Johns Hopkins University, where his students included James and Dewey.

As indicated above, Peirce believed that there was much more to the universe than its mechanical aspects, and that ultimately there was no separation between mind and body. He believed that individuals were interdependent with their environment, including different levels of community. Concerning evolution—physical (including biological) and social, he was convinced that mechanical and chance (i.e., natural selection) approaches, while having some limited usefulness, missed the main evolutionary force.[142] Peirce stressed "agapastic evolution" in which love in the form of sympathetic understanding, as in the Greek concept of *agape*, was the prime mover of evolution through the intelligibility of the cosmos and the continuity of "minds" participating in the process of change.

On the social level, he rejected the survival-of-the-fittest ideas of social Darwinism that made a virtue out of greed. In one comment, he begins sarcastically:

> Intelligence in the service of greed ensures the justest of prices, the fairest contracts, the most enlightened conduct of all dealing between men, and leads to the *sumum bonum*, food in plenty and comfort. Food for whom? For the greedy master of intelligence.
>
> What I say, then, is that the great attention paid to economical questions during our century has induced an exaggeration of the beneficial effects of greed and the unfortunate results of sentiment, until there has resulted a philosophy which comes unwittingly to this, that greed is the great agent in the elevation of the human race and the evolution of the universe.[143]

So a miser is a beneficent power in a community, is he? With the same reason precisely, only to a much higher degree, you might pronounce the Wall Street sharp to be a good angel, who takes money from heedless persons not likely to guard it properly, who wrecks feeble enterprises better stopped, ... and who by a thousand wiles puts money at the service of intelligent greed, in his own person.[144]

For Peirce, life at its most basic level was not a competition between separate individuals, but he believed that:

progress comes with every individual merging his individual differences with his neighbors.[145]

It is indicative of Peirce's outlook that his first wife of twenty-one years was Melusina Fay, a leader in the cooperative housekeeping movement. Quite consistent with Native American ways of seeing, though mixing in numerous other strands of thought in his own creative thinking, he saw life as relational. His perspective was also consistent with Indian ways concerning character-developing education, and continuing learning and growth. For him, all things, including the universe itself, tended to develop habits and proceed on their basis, learning and, thus growing, with unfolding experience: "The existence of things consists in their regular behavior."[146]

His view is that the process of interaction brings about movement for change, including change of habit, or regular behavior. For thinking human beings, individually and collectively, living in a universe at a stage in which both natural law and chance function, the proper approach is to apply science to experience. In other words, one should reflect upon developing events so as to consciously modify habits to meet changing circumstances. In his era, that meant, among other things, society moving from valuing greed to returning to honoring a caring reciprocity.

John Dewey, Democrat and Progressive Educator

John Dewey was born to a family of modest means in Burlington, Vermont, in 1859.[147] He graduated from the University of Vermont, then taught high school for two years in Oil City, Pennsylvania, and elementary school in Charlotte, Vermont. Following this, he studied at Johns Hopkins University, taking some courses from Charles Sanders Peirce, as did William James. Dewey is considered one of the founders of the philosophy of pragmatism and of American psychology. His major work encompassed participatory, as opposed to representative, democracy and education, where he was a major voice in progressive education. Among other achievements, while on the faculty of the University of Chicago, he founded the University of Chicago Laboratory School, a model in progressive education. He also produced important work in other areas, including in epistemology, metaphysics, aesthetics, art, logic, social theory, and ethics.

Consistent with his belief that there should be no separation between thought and action, and that the philosopher needed to be active in the community, Dewey was an activist on many issues. He was a public philosopher, speaking regularly on social issues and promoting well-working democracy, while encouraging fellow philosophers to apply their profession in public discussion and action:

> If philosophy does not embrace the process of growth as the guide to knowledge, truth and ethics, it will fall into the apathy of irrelevance.[148]

He served on the board of Hull House, helped immigrants in Chicago, worked for women's suffrage, and was active as a reformer in education. Dewey was also a vocal progressive on public issues. This reflected his views on diversity. He opposed the idea that America was, or should be, a melting pot, helping pave the way for the multiculturalism that arose in the mainstream late in the twentieth century.

Dewey emphasized the importance of the interchange of ideas in robust public discussion by an informed citizenry, of diverse people. He found, "Uniformity and unanimity in culture rather repellant," noting:

> Variety is the spice of life, and the richness and attractiveness of social institutions depend upon cultural diversity of separate units. In so far as people are all alike, there is no give and take among them.[149]

In his view, only with open interaction was individual and social growth sufficiently attainable. This required that people be reflective and open-minded, traits which needed to be encouraged by a progressive education. This kind of education recognizes and works with the differences in young people, with student-centered supported learning, providing the maximum number of positive experiences in which the student participates as an active learner, examining situations and issues from as many viewpoints as practicable. Dewey's aim is to free the student and the society, recognizing that:

> freedom is found in that kind of interaction which maintains an environment in which human desire and choice count for something.[150]

A deeper discussion of what progressive education is about is presented with examples in chapter 8, "Facilitating the Unfolding of the Circle: Indigenizing Education for the Twenty-First Century."

Dewey's views of democracy and education are intimately related to the understanding he developed of human psychology. In accordance with the four conceptions of pragmatism, psychology and psychological development are not merely individual. They involve the interaction of the individual with his or her unique combination of qualities and their environment. Dewey expresses that it is in the course of this interaction that the mind develops, forming habits in reaction to experience:

> Habits may be profitably compared to physiological functions, like breathing, digesting. The latter, are to be sure, involuntary, while habits are acquired.... Walking implicates the ground as well as the legs; speech demands physical air and human companionship ... natural operations ... and acquired ones like speech and honesty are functions of the surroundings as truly as of the person. They are things done by the environment by means of organic structures or acquired dispensations.... They involve skill of sensory and motor organs, cunning or craft, and objective materials. They assimilate objective energies, and eventuate in command of the environment.... They have a beginning, middle and end.[151]

Further, his beliefs included that habits are only relatively fixed and can be changed by ongoing experience. Hence the nature of that experience is important. A particularly helpful development is if that experience encourages the development of an analytic, in a sense scientific, consciousness. This allows one to evaluate behavior in light of new experience. Habits normally function largely unconsciously, and it is impossible to remain continually fully aware of them. But if the habit of reflection is developed, then one is able to become constructively conscious of habits when experience indicates that they may no longer be appropriate and lead to positive growth.

Dewey also believed that in traditional societies intimately relating with their natural environments, the experiences of human development generally unfolded sufficiently naturally so that most people evolved good habits for their communal situations. He was concerned that in modern societies, more isolated from their natural physical environment, and in several dimensions having gotten artificially out of balance, the process of evolving appropriate habits had become defective. He writes:

> We have at present little or next to no controlled art of securing that redirection of behavior which constitutes adequate perception or consciousness. That is, we have little or no art of education in the fundamentals, namely in the management of organic attitudes which color the qualities of our conscious objects and acts. As long as our chief psycho-physical coordinations are formed blindly and in the dark during infancy and early childhood, they are accidental adjustments to the pressure of other persons and circumstances which act upon us. They do not then take into account the consequences of these activities upon formation of habits.... Hence the connection between consciousness and action is precarious, and its possession a doubtful boon as compared with the efficacy of instinct—or structure—in lower animals.[152]

Out of this persuasion, Dewey worked for education and societal reform.

The Native Roots of Classical Progressivism

With Dewey's pragmatic philosophy and progressive education, one can draw a direct line back to the American Indian sources that ultimately influenced his thinking, a line that is also evident in the thoughts of James and Peirce.[153] Dewey states clearly in *John Dewey Presents the Living Thought of Thomas Jefferson*[154] that he admires, as anticipating pragmatism, Jefferson's Indian-influenced experimental attitude toward democracy with a commitment to growth. Dewey similarly states that he finds in Jefferson the experimentalism of eighteenth-century science which he incorporates in pragmatism. That scientific experimentalism was developed more by Jefferson's colleague Benjamin Franklin, but it was furthered greatly by Jefferson, as well.

Dewey makes clear in *Living Thought of Thomas Jefferson* that Franklin was the greater exponent of a Native-influenced science. Dewey there quotes Jefferson that Franklin was "the greatest man and ornament of the age and country in which he lived (p. 28)." Dewey admits:

There was no discovery in natural science to the credit of Jefferson similar to that of Franklin in electricity. (p. 6)

In continuing, Dewey gives a clue his reason for presenting Jefferson rather than Franklin:

But his faith in scientific advance as a means of popular enlightenment and of social progress was backed by a continual interest in discoveries made by others. (p. 6)

Jefferson's Indian-like, and to a considerable degree Indian-influenced, views of nature, experience, the need for continued reexamination and learning, and democracy are all central to Dewey, who while an independent thinker, was part of the same Indigenous-impacted tradition as his predecessor. Thus, Dewey quotes Jefferson:

To illustrate what I believe to be the key to the work and character of our first great democrat: the vital union of attitudes and convictions so spontaneous that they are the kind called instinctive with fruits of a rich and varied experience:—a union that was cemented by the ceaseless intellectual activity which was his "supreme delight." But in a more conventional way, he was that rare person in politics, an idealist whose native faith was developed, checked, and confirmed by extremely extensive and varied practical experience. It is seldom, I imagine, that an unusually sincere and unified natural temperament has been so happily combined with rich opportunities for observation and reflection. If he left the stamp of idealism upon the course of events, it is because this experience added realistic substance to the inherent bent of his natural disposition. (pp. 2–3)

A more direct line of Indian influence on Dewey came through Lydia Maria Child, who lived until 1880 and continued to publish until 1878, including *An Appeal for Indians* in 1868. Child and her colleagues in the women's suffrage movement were known to Dewey through his activity at Hull House, where he also met Indians and African American rights activists, who included many women's suffrage advocates. Comparisons of Child's writings with those of Dewey and James's show many striking similarities. It is clear that from Child and her successors, as Pratt writes in *Native Pragmatism*:

The classical pragmatists, and Dewey in particular, learned from them to apply the abstract conceptions of science and democracy to the lived experience of a pluralistic society in which diversity of groups, interests and ideas could coexist. In the end, classical pragmatism and its four commitments emerge from a complex environment characterized by both colonial and Indigenous attitudes. What is generally recognized as a distinctly American philosophy arises from the influences of both European and Indian thought on key figures throughout the Seventeenth, Eighteenth and Nineteenth Centuries. In the end, pragmatism becomes more than the development of a particular philosophy. It becomes a genealogy of a rich American philosophical tradition—diverse in its thinkers, plural in its traditions, and potentially valuable in its implications for life in a multicultural world.[155]

The Continuing Pragmatist Tradition

With the firm establishment of classical pragmatism in the United States by Peirce, James, Dewey, Adams, Royce, George Herbert

Mead, and others writing and acting well into the twentieth century, American pragmatism became a major force in public thinking and in the field of philosophy in the United States. As discussed in *American Philosophy from Wounded Knee to the Present* by McKenna and Pratt, pragmatism, with some ups and downs, has continued to expand in the United States with broader worldwide implications up to the present moment. In some instances the development has remained very much in the classical pragmatist tradition. In others pragmatism has interacted and interwoven with other ways of thinking to form a broader American philosophy of which pragmatism, or some of its aspects, are elements. Some pieces or works of pragmatism have gone off on their own, intermingling with other ways of seeing.

An example of this is Peirce's semiotics, which became an independent field with numerous branches and approaches extending beyond philosophy into such areas as linguistics and anthropology, often being approached in ways that were quite contrary to classical pragmatism's four conceptions. These strands of thinking, however, reconnected the pragmatist tradition with the analysis and writing of such philosophers as W. V. O. Quine and C. J. Ducasse.[156]

As Cornell West states in the discussion of the African American connection above, since the early twentieth century there has been quite a range of approaches and views that have been considered at least somewhat pragmatist. Some of them, and those who expressed them, have kept to the socially conscious and activist American Indian equalitarian pluralism that is at the heart of pragmatism. Horace Kallen, one of the founders of the New School for Social Research, along with Dewey and Alain LeRoy Locke, for instance, early in the twentieth century wrote and acted against racism and for cultural pluralism.[157] Later in the century activists for inclusive diversity included Richard Wright and Martin Luther King Jr.[158] Wright wrote the book *Black Power* in 1954; it is the first publicly known use of that term. He argued that the concept of race was a dualistic invention used to divide people. Martin Luther King Jr., while at Boston University, had studied with professors working in the pragmatist tradition. At times, he reflected what he had learned in that tradition, as with saying, following Royce, that all people were members of "the beloved community."

Similarly, among the social critics working from a pragmatist background were sociologist C. Wright Mills, writer Lewis Mumford, and economist John Kenneth Galbraith.[159] Mills's critiques of the "power elite," and the accompanying increasing disempowerment of the middle and lower classes, were developed against the background of his knowledge of the work of Peirce, Dewey, and Mead, along with his reading of Thorstein Veblen's *The Leisure Class*, written in 1899.

Mumford, whose education included studies at the New School for Social Research, and who at times mentioned Dewey, wrote more than thirty books and one thousand essays applying "usable history" to illuminate the sources of contemporary problems. In addition to his writing, Mumford was an active voice against McCarthyism and highway projects that would damage neighborhoods and people. He also spoke for nuclear disarmament.

Galbraith continued into the twenty-first century to be a vocal critic of the concentration of economic power and policies that fostered it. He wrote numerous books on economics, and served US presidents on and off from Franklin Roosevelt to George H. W. Bush. His economic writings were largely focused on practical policy aimed at promoting economic equality. Also in the pragmatist tradition, he emphasized the need for independent thinking and interchange of ideas. Some of his economic commentary is discussed in chapter 6 of this volume.

Philosophical ideas that can be used as standards to critique existing conditions can also be applied to justify conditions that do not live up to the cited standard. That certainly has been the case for some pragmatist ideas. Pluralism and democracy are good examples.

Some well-to-do people and agents of powerful interests have often defended the unequal status quo, claiming that the United States functions extremely fairly because it is democratic, with everyone having a say in a pluralist society. There are cases also of people, including philosophers, who on theoretical issues take positions in the pragmatist tradition, quoting some of its adherents, but who do not apply them to analyzing social issues.

One who has been partly in this position is philosopher Richard Rorty.[160] Writing both academically and popularly, Rorty did much in the late twentieth and early twenty-first centuries to increase the already expanding interest in pragmatism. He has often taken clear general stands on major public issues, including opposition to the Vietnam War. But Rorty has been criticized for offering little in the way of policy or action proposals for addressing concrete problems.

Meanwhile, the trend of pragmatism interacting with related activisms that long proceeded the rise of classical pragmatism has continued, and in some instances expanded. Its continuing connection to the civil rights movement has already been mentioned. Pragmatism has also remained connected with the ongoing women's movement, some of whose direct Indian connections are discussed below. Meanwhile, there has been continued significant new input from American Indians. This has been especially the case in the rise of the environmental movement discussed below.

Pragmatic thinking has also included the rise of broadly important Native writers, including Vine Deloria Jr., and the launching of an American Indian Philosophy Association that meets at the conferences of the American Philosophical Association, while facilitating collaborative publishing.[161] Moreover, since the 1950s, there has been a great increase in public interest in American Indians, and in the impact of American Indian writers and filmmakers across a number of fields and upon the general public, discussed below and in the introduction to part II. These developments have made contributions to the American philosophy of pragmatism.

The first two decades of the twenty-first century have continued to experience an expansion of pragmatism in the field of philosophy, and in public officials, at least on one side, in an increasingly polarized United States.[162] An example within philosophy of a writer with public impact is Richard Bernstein. Among his many writings on important public concerns is the *Abuse of Evil: The Corruption of Politics and Religion since 9/11*,[163] published in 2005. In responding to public and government reactions to the 2011 al-Qaeda attacks on the World Trade Towers in New York City and the Pentagon, Bernstein comments:

> Responsible Choices and actions always demand specificity, sensitivity to context, careful analysis, clarification of real options, debate and persuasion. But it doesn't follow that there is nothing to be done.... In times of widespread anxiety, fear, and perceived crisis, there is a craving for absolutes, firm moral certainties, and simplistic schemas that help make sense of confusing contingencies; they help to provide a sense of psychological security. Since 9/11 we have been living though such a time.... The careless talk of evil and the demonizing of our enemies do not help matters. On the contrary—as I have argued—they obscure complex issues, block enquiry, and stifle public debate about appropriate responses to an unsettling, fluid state of affairs. So what is to be done? Ordinary citizens must stand up and oppose the political abuse of evil, challenge the misuse of absolutes, expose false and misleading claims to moral certainty, and argue that we cannot deal with the complexity of the issues we confront by appealing to—or imposing—simplistic dichotomies. There is a role for public intellectuals, educators, journalists, and artists to help guide the way— just as Holmes, James, Peirce and Dewey did at a different time under radically different historical circumstance.[164]

Among the public officials of the early twenty-first century, often acting in the public interest quite consistently with the pragmatist principles to which Bernstein referred, has been Barack Obama.[165] While he may be faulted for too much secrecy and closed-door decision-making on some intelligence and military issues, as president Obama most often stood for open discussion of issues and for the making of decisions based upon well-determined facts and carefully analyzed policy. If he can be criticized for being too slow to act on some issues, he was at least open to learning from his own and the nation's experience as illustrated by his change of mind to support gay marriage. In his remarks on the Supreme Court's decision in favor of marriage equality, he expresses both the principles of diversity, and of growth through public learning, while dealing with specific problems in their context:

> Good morning. Our nation was founded on a bedrock principle that we are all created equal. The project of each generation is to bridge the meaning of those founding words with the realities of changing times—a never-ending quest to ensure those words ring true for every single American.
>
> Progress on this journey often comes in small increments, sometimes two steps forward, one step back, propelled by the persistent effort of dedicated citizens. And then sometimes, there are days like this when that slow, steady effort is rewarded with justice that arrives like a thunderbolt.
>
> This morning, the Supreme Court recognized that the Constitution guarantees marriage equality. In doing so, they've reaffirmed that all Americans are entitled to the equal protection of the law. That all people should be treated equally, regardless of who they are or who they love.
>
> This decision will end the patchwork system we currently have. It will end the uncertainty hundreds of thousands of same-sex couples face from not knowing whether their marriage, legitimate in the eyes of one state, will remain if they decide to move [to] or even visit another. This ruling will strengthen all of our communities by offering to all loving same-sex couples the dignity of marriage across this great land.
>
> In my second inaugural address, I said that if we are truly created equal, then surely the love we commit to one

another must be equal as well. It is gratifying to see that principle enshrined into law by this decision....

I know change for many of our LGBT brothers and sisters must have seemed so slow for so long. But compared to so many other issues, America's shift has been so quick. I know that Americans of goodwill continue to hold a wide range of views on this issue. Opposition in some cases has been based on sincere and deeply held beliefs. All of us who welcome today's news should be mindful of that fact; recognize different viewpoints; revere our deep commitment to religious freedom.

But today should also give us hope that on the many issues with which we grapple, often painfully, real change is possible. Shifts in hearts and minds is possible. And those who have come so far on their journey to equality have a responsibility to reach back and help others join them. Because for all our differences, we are one people, stronger together than we could ever be alone. That's always been our story.[166]

Obama's quite pragmatistic statement has roots in his early experience and education.[167] Born in Hawai'i in 1961, he had a multicultural upbringing. His mother, Ann Dunham, was a white woman from Kansas with English, Welsh, Scottish, Irish, German, and Swiss ancestry. His father, Barack Obama Sr., was from Kenya. Dunham and Obama Sr. were divorced in 1964, and Dunham married Lolo Soetoro from Indonesia in 1965. From ages six through ten he lived with his parents in Indonesia, attended a Catholic school for two years, and a public school for a year and a half to supplement his home schooling in English by his mother. He returned to Hawai'i in 1971 where he attended a private high school. He alternated living with his mother while she completed a degree in anthropology with living with his maternal grandparents, particularly in 1975 when his mother returned to Indonesia to undertake fieldwork. Obama says of his years in Hawai'i:

The opportunity that Hawai'i offered—to experience a variety of cultures in a climate of mutual respect—became an integral part of my world view, and a basis for the values I hold most dear.[168]

While at college at Columbia University, Obama's studies included James, Dewey, Du Bois, and Locke. At Harvard Law School, he took a class from Brazilian pragmatist Roberto Unger. As president of the *Harvard Law Review,* he regularly oversaw the publication of issues with articles by pragmatist philosophers including Richard Bernstein and Hilary Putnam. Later, his work as a community organizer in Chicago built on the ideas of Addams and Hull House, while teaching him the importance of listening, both to those in need and to those with differing viewpoints. Thus Obama had a firm foundation for being one of the leaders of an expanding pragmatism in action, with its American Indian roots, in the twenty-first century.

In examining the Indian influences on the American philosophy of pragmatism, and the broader American philosophy of which it is a part, it is important to remember that Indigenous thinking is only one of the important sets of often, but not always, interacting strands that have contributed to these philosophical traditions. As McKenna and Pratt have developed in *American Philosophy: From Wounded Knee to the Present,* the diverse strands within the American philosophy of resistance have sometimes dialogued with each other, and sometimes; though at times even when they have not directly interacted there have been indirect influences.

In addition, there have been movements against, or otherwise less open to, Native ways of seeing. This is clear in examining the polarization in thinking in the United States today, discussed in the early portions of part II of this volume. As Pratt and McKenna have indicated, and Pratt communicated to Stephen Sachs:

Intellectual developments after the Civil War made indigenous thought something that was reacted against in the process of formulating a new conception of agency that became the dominant conception of agency in the 20th century.

Thus American Indian thinking has had, and continues to have, an extremely important influence, but it is only one of the continually changing strands in the ever developing fabric of thought in the United States and beyond.

Section 3: "Sovereign Women in a Sovereign Nation"

Sally Roesch Wagner

The huge impact of the full equality of women in American Indian societies upon the women's movement in the United States, beginning in the nineteenth century, is no longer widely known, even among women in the movement. That was the case with this author, until I began to spend considerable time in Indian country.

"Sovereign women in a sovereign nation." I first heard the phrase from the late Tillie Black Bear, a Sicangu Lakota founder of the White Buffalo Calf Woman Society Inc. on Rosebud Reservation, the first battered women's shelter on a Native nation.

I gratefully accepted it as a gift, another mentor phrase, a portal into a deeper understanding of Indigenous culture and the extraordinary (by non-Native standards) position women have historically held within the First Nations. It joined concepts like the Haudenosaunee describing the unborn as "the faces still in the ground" and "women and the earth are one and the same." These thoughts act as my intellectual GPS to enter into a world that I, as an outsider, will only ever imperfectly comprehend, but the degree to which I can follow the directions I am changed. Transformed might not be too strong a term. In the process, I am always aware of how I am a feminist repeating history.

I began this journey that ended up in Indian country when I was trying to understand how the most radical, far-thinking of the United States suffragists, Matilda Joslyn Gage, came to envision a world not of equality, but of total social transformation. The road quickly led to the Haudenosaunee—the five nations of the "Iroquois" confederacy: the Mohawk, Oneida, Onondaga, Cayuga, and Seneca; later joined by the Tuscarora. Gage, who was the third member of the National Woman Suffrage Association leadership triumvirate with Susan B. Anthony and Elizabeth Cady Stanton, pointed to the Haudenosaunee as a continuing example of the pre-patriarchal, woman-empowered, peaceful, egalitarian social structure of society. "Never was justice more perfect; never was civilization higher," she wrote in her magnum opus, *Woman, Church and State,* in 1893.[169] Christianity upset the applecart with its Eve-as-bringer-of-evil mythology, she charged, requiring women to be under the divinely-decreed authority of men as punishment.

Reading this powerful pronouncement, I was disbelieving and disoriented. Didn't I have one of the first doctorates awarded for work in women's studies in the United States? Wasn't I a founder of one of the first academic women's studies programs? And didn't I know more about Matilda Joslyn Gage than any living soul, having resurrected her from obscurity, written out of history for her radicalness as she was?[170] She couldn't have been influenced by American Indian women, or I would have known this.

The mentor phrase that lifted me out of my crazy feeling and stabilized me into research came from Paula Gunn Allen (Laguna Pueblo) in her important work *The Sacred Hoop: Recovering the Feminine in American Indian Traditions.* Allen couldn't have more clearly described my position:

> Feminists too often believe that no one has ever experienced the kind of society that empowered women and made that empowerment the basis of its rules and civilization. The price the feminist community must pay because it is not aware of the recent presence of gynarchical societies on this

continent is unnecessary confusion, division, and much lost time.... The root of oppression is the loss of memory....

As I write this, I am aware of how far removed my version of the roots of American feminism must seem to those steeped in either mainstream or radical versions of feminism's history... I am intensely conscious of popular notions of Indian women as beasts of burden, squaws, traitors, or, at best, vanished denizens of a long-lost wilderness. How odd, then, must my contention seem that the gynocratic tribes of the American continent provided the basis for all the dreams of liberation that characterize the modern world.[171]

The root of oppression is the loss of memory. That was what I needed to get my mind around. I understood getting to the root of the problem; that was a common nineteenth-century activist adage. Like a tree, which only grows stronger if you trim its branches, minor reform like the vote only makes the system of oppression stronger. No, the way to end this oppression is an immediate, unconditional end to women's subordinate position. We must dig out the very roots of the institution: from rewriting the Bible to rethinking what it means to be a man or a woman, Matilda Joslyn Gage believed. Hence, radical. At the root. Using the common analogy of a poisonous tree, abolitionist Frederick Douglass declared that "The deadly upas, root and branch, leaf and fibre, body and sap, must be utterly destroyed," if slavery was to be abolished.[172]

I also understood the loss of memory. I knew the arduous journey of reclaiming memories that had been long suppressed through a powerfully effective, but inherently unhealthy, survival mechanism—both personally and culturally. Having been down the road to recover memory of my own past, I had guideposts to help me travel on the journey to reclaim memory of my feminist past.

I started with the easiest, most highly traveled four-lane feminist highway to our political past: the law. Journeying to the source of the legal rights that women have won since we organized officially

in the nineteenth century, I found Indigenous influence everywhere hidden in plain sight.[173]

The position of women under United States law was grim from
the beginning, when the founding fathers (against Abigail Adams's
warning) decided to follow England's interpretation of common
law, which denied women legal personhood. "The two shall become
one and the one is the man," intoned the church, and common
law followed by legislating this subordinate position of women.
Married women were considered dead in the eyes of US and state
law, and they had no legal existence; the wife and mother was the
virtual slave of her husband. Not all men were tyrants; but the law,
as Lucretia Mott said, gave all men the right of tyranny.

Nor did women have many options. Under this system, marriage
became employment, the one job open to most women when all but
a few other means of employment were closed to them and the few
available ones paid half, or less, of the wages men were paid for
the same work. As Elizabeth Cady Stanton and her Quaker friends
wrote in the movement's founding document, the "Declaration
of Sentiments," penned for what may have been the first women's
rights convention in the world's history, held the summer of 1848
in Seneca Falls, New York:

> He has made her, if married, in the eye of the law, civilly
> dead.
>
> He has taken from her all right in property, even to the
> wages she earns.
>
> In the covenant of marriage, she is compelled to promise
> obedience to her husband, he becoming, to all intents and
> purposes, her master—the law giving him power to deprive
> her of her liberty, and to administer chastisement.[174]

This was not injustice, the chorus of government, religion,
science, economics, and the family all agreed. This second-class
position of women was both natural and divinely inspired, all
institutions intoned. Women were weak—physically, mentally,

spiritually, and emotionally—clinging vines needing the sturdy oak of their fathers, and then their husbands, for support. God made Adam first, then Eve as a helpmate. When she disobeyed His law, God put her under the authority of men as punishment, the theological reasoning went. When women rose up to demand treatment equal to that of men, they were accused of violating God's edict and nature's mandate.

How to break through this monolithic voice of oppression? If there was one culture in which women had an equal status to men, women could put the lie to the biological and theological imperative that dictated the tight boundaries of their lives. What they found was that just such a culture wasn't some mythological matriarchal dream of a long-forgotten past. It lived next door.

Matilda Joslyn Gage was well aware of her Haudenosaunee neighbors. While president of the National Woman Suffrage Association in 1875, she wrote a series of front-page stories for the *New York Evening Post*. The newspaper editor introduced the series to his readers by observing that Gage expressed "an exhibition of ardent devotion to the cause of women's rights which is very proper in the president of the…Suffrage Association and gives prominence to the fact that in the old days when the glory of the famous [Haudenosaunee] confederation…was at its height, the power and importance of women were recognized by the allied tribes."[175]

In these articles, other newspaper and journal articles, the woman's rights newspaper she edited (*The National Citizen and Ballot Box*, 1878–1881), and her major work (*Woman, Church and State*, 1893), Gage lauded the Six Nations of the Haudenosaunee confederacy. Over a twenty-year period, she noted especially the position of women in what she termed their "matriarchate" or system of "mother-rule." "Under their women," she wrote, "the science of government reached the highest form known to the world."[176] This was the gynocracy that Allen wrote about! Civilization reached its zenith in these egalitarian, peaceful, and balanced nations, in which women held responsibilities of equal importance with men but also, along with Mother Earth, held the sacred responsibility of creating life, Gage believed. Gage continued her writing about the Haudenosaunee until the end of her life—she was working on a book about the Six Nations when she died in 1898.[177]

Gage was not the only suffragist who lauded the superior position of Indigenous women. When the early feminists (including Stanton, Anthony, and Gage) gathered for the first time internationally to discuss their issues in 1888, Alice Fletcher addressed the International Council of Women with a remarkable story from her work as an ethnographer. She was living in the home of a woman on the Omaha nation. One day this woman gave away a fine quality horse. Alice was startled, she reported, because she had heard no family discussion about it. "Will your husband like to have you give the horse away?" asked Alice. Her hostess's "eyes danced," Fletcher told the suffragist convention and, "breaking into a peal of laughter, she hastened to tell the story to the other women gathered in the tent, and I became the target of many merry eyes." In vain Fletcher "tried to explain how a white woman would act," but "laughter and contempt met my explanation of the white man's hold upon his wife's property."[178]

Her attempts to explain the laws which denied property, and even legal existence, to white women, Fletcher told the feminist conference, were "met with but one response" from Native women. They said: "As an Indian woman I was free. I owned my home, my person, the work of my own hands, and my children could never forget me. I was better as an Indian woman than under white law."[179]

Agriculture, for one thing, was women's responsibility, and they developed a method entirely different from "our own"—and far superior, Gage informed her readers. "In olden Iroquois tillage there was no turning the sod with a plough to which were harnessed a cow and a woman, as is seen today in Christian Germany," she wryly commented. The ground was literally "tickled with a hoe" and it "laughed with a harvest." Corn, the "great staple," was planted in mounds and "but little labor attended its cultivation."[180] And what an abundance! They raised corn, beans, and squash, the Three Sisters, which, eaten together, constitute a nutritionally balanced food group. The Three Sisters also work together ecologically. The corn stalk provides support for the beans while the beans provide nitrogen for the corn. The squash covers the mound, keeping weeds out and moisture in.

"DO YOU LOVE CORN?" Matilda Joslyn Gage's question caught the eye of readers picking up the *New York Evening Mail* on November 3, 1875. If so, she had no doubt they would want to "bless the man" who invented the national corn dish, that "luscious mixture of green corn, beans, and venison"—succotash. She had a surprise in store for her audience, however. Succotash—"correctly called msickquatash"—was given to us by Haudenosaunee women, and "you cannot deprive my sex of that glory," she admonished. After replacing the venison with pork and changing the name, she went on, "we white people speak of it as one of our national dishes." Nor was it the only "culinary remembrance of the red-woman's skill in cookery," either, for "more than one of our national dishes is ours not by invention, but by adoption from our Indian predecessors."[181]

Gage was similarly impressed by the spiritual sophistication of the Haudenosaunee, writing that "three of the five ancient feasts of the Iroquois were agricultural feasts connected with this, their great staple." "Centuries ago," she admired, "was agriculture honored by this ancient people."[182] This recognition of the spiritual, life-giving supremacy of woman's creation of food represented to Gage a higher form of civilization than her own:

In Christian Europe during the [M]iddle [A]ges, the agriculturalist was despised; the warrior was the aristocrat of civilization. In publicly honoring agriculture as did the Ongwe Honwe[183] three times a year, they surpassed in wisdom the men of Europe.[184]

Mother Earth and women were one and the same creators of life, which was why Haudenosaunee women had responsibility for the land. As Gage wrote:

No sale of lands was valid without consent of the [women] and among the State Archives at Albany, New York, treaties are preserved signed by the "Sachems and Principal Women of the Six Nations."[185]

Gage marveled at Haudenosaunee women's authority in the "family relation":

When an Indian husband brought the products of the chase to the wigwam,[186] his control over it ceased. In the home, the wife was absolute; the sale of the skins was regulated by her, the price was paid to her.[187]

Women's responsibility for food extended from the land on which it was grown to the growing of it, through to its distribution and its creation into an edible form. This resulted in "woman's superiority in power" in the home, Gage wrote. US women, on the other hand, had no legally recognized authority in the home, and no economic power—everything women brought into their marriage or earned became the property of their husbands. They did not "own" the food they cooked, the pot they cooked it in, the plates they served it on or the house they cooked it in.

Judith Brown, a modern anthropologist, goes beyond Gage, suggesting that, as Haudenosaunee women:

controlled the factors of agricultural production [and] maintained the *right* to distribute and dispense all food, even that procured by men, [they controlled the] economic organization [not just of the home, but] of the tribe.[188]

While the Western language of hierarchy—superiority, control, power—does not have meaning in an egalitarian society, both Gage and Brown, in their culturally biased way, are reflecting women's authority and responsibility, which was balanced by men's responsibility for diplomacy, security, and hunting.

Another contrast feminists recognized between their legal position and that of Haudenosaunee women was their authority as mothers. Women under most state laws had no right to the children that they birthed. As Gage explained in 1871:

Blackstone, the chief exponent of common law, says: "A mother has no legal right or authority over her children; she is only entitled to respect and honor." The United States, governing itself by English law, inherited this with other oppressions, and it to this day holds force in most of the thirty-seven States of the Union.[189]

These laws, Gage wrote, even permitted:

the dying father of an unborn child to will it away, and to give any person he pleases to select the right to wait the advent of that child, and when the mother, at the hazard of her own life, has brought it forth, to rob her of it and to do by it as the dead father directed.[190]

The New York law, for example read:

Every father, whether of full age or a minor, of a child likely to be born, or of any living child under the age of twenty-one years and unmarried, may, by his deed or last will duly executed, dispose of the custody and tuition of such child, during its minority, or for any less time, to any person or persons in possession or remainder.[191]

An enraged Gage exploded:

What an anomaly on Justice is such a law! ... "It is better to be a live dog than a dead lion," was a proverb I learned in my childhood—but I have learned a new rendering: "It is better to be a dead father than a live mother."[192]

Haudenosaunee women lived the opposite reality. Born of their mother into her clan, the children followed their mother's line. The living arrangements were based on this matrilineal system. Upon marriage, a husband came to live with his wife, her parents, her sisters, and their children and husbands in their matrilineal family longhouse. When the brothers married, they moved to their wives' longhouses. If any of the mothers died, their children stayed in the longhouse and were raised by their matrilineal family. If the couple split, the children also stayed with their mother and her family. Gage wrote about the recognition of the primacy of the mother-child bond among the Haudenosaunee:

> If for any cause the Iroquois husband and wife separated, the wife took with her all the property she had brought into the wigwam; the children also accompanied the mother, whose right to them was recognized as supreme.[193]

Violence against women was legally sanctioned under US law. Husbands had the right to beat their wives, as Sir William Blackstone explained in his 1760s *Commentaries on the Laws of England,* which codified English common law:

> [Since the husband] is to answer for her misbehavior, the law thought it reasonable to intrust him with this power of restraining her, by domestic chastisement, in the same moderation that a man is allowed to correct his apprentices or children.[194]

The North Carolina Supreme Court followed this interpretation in 1852 in a case where the judge:

> instructed the jury, that by law the husband had a right to give his wife moderate correction, if it appears to be necessary to enforce obedience to his lawful command, but no right to beat her from mere wantonness and wickedness.[195]

And again, in 1864 the North Carolina Supreme Court further clarified:

A husband cannot be convicted of a battery on his wife unless he inflicts a permanent injury or uses such excessive violence or cruelty as indicates malignity or vindictiveness; and it makes no difference that the husband and wife are living separate by agreement.[196]

In both cases, the batterers were found innocent.
In another case four years later, when the court found that:

the defendant struck Elizabeth Rhodes, his wife, three licks, with a switch about the size of one of his fingers (but not as large as a man's thumb), without any provocation except some words uttered by her and not recollected by the witness, [the judge] was of opinion that the defendant had a right to whip his wife with a switch no larger than his thumb, and that upon the facts found in the special verdict he was not guilty in law.[197]

Women who found themselves married to an abusive husband were trapped, legally as well as economically, because divorce laws were extremely rigid. Conditions had regressed from earlier times, when Europeans living closely with Indians had been inspired to take on some of their ways, as is discussed in chapter 1. Colonial New England allowed more grounds for divorce than New York State possessed in the 1960s. There was no organized underground railroad to help married women escape, such as existed for African Americans, and many were the stories of runaway wives being tracked-down and brought home to their husbands by the local sheriff. Their legal oppression deepening after the American Revolution; women, who had voted in some of the colonies, were at the same time robbed of the ballot—the legal means of securing their rights.[198]

Again, the suffragists pointed out the huge contrast between the liberty of United States and Haudenosaunee women. In a speech before the National Council of Women in 1891, Elizabeth Cady Stanton drew from the memoirs of Ashur Wright, a long-time missionary among the Seneca, who related:

> Usually the females ruled the house. The stores were in common; but woe to the luckless husband or lover who was too shiftless to do his share of the providing. No matter how many children, or whatever goods he might have in the house, he might at any time be ordered to pick up his blanket and budge; and after such an order it would not be healthful for him to attempt to disobey. The house would be too hot for him; and unless saved by the intercession of some aunt or grandmother he must retreat to his own clan, or go and start a new matrimonial alliance in some other.[199]

Stanton was especially sensitive to this issue of divorce. While not supported by all suffragists, she was courageous in advocating that the laws be changed to allow women the right to leave "disagreeable" marriages. For this stand, she was labeled an infidel by Christian denominations which generally held that marriage was a covenant with God which no woman had a right to break, even if her life was in danger from a violent husband. She countered:

> If marriage cannot be dissolved and man's authority, according to God's law, is absolute in that relation, women who enter it are either fools or ignorant of the laws that govern it.[200]

When Alice Fletcher spoke to the International Council of Women in 1888, she explained that wife battering was not condoned and, when it occurred, was dealt with in Native nations:

The wife never becomes entirely under the control of her husband. Her kindred have a prior right, and can use that right to separate her from him or to protect her from him, should he maltreat her. The brother who would not rally to the help of his sister would become a by-word among his clan. Not only will he protect her at the risk of his life from insult and injury, but he will seek help for her when she is sick and suffering.[201]

Violence against women, endemic among men in the United States, was a behavior seldom seen among the Haudenosaunee, and when it occurred, was dealt with harshly. Non-Native women experienced a personal safety on Native nations that they never knew—in their homes or out—on their own soil. "It shows the remarkable security of living on an Indian Reservation, that a solitary woman can walk about for miles, at any hour of the day or night, in perfect safety," school teacher Mary Elizabeth Beauchamp remarked in a letter to the *Skaneateles Democrat*.[202]

"I'll tell you another thing too, that may be hard to believe, though it is as true as gospel," a white mail carrier told a New York *Herald* reporter who was doing a story on the Haudenosaunee. "A white woman can go around alone among them or on the most desolate roads with perfect safety. I'd rather have my wife or daughter go around alone at night in this reservation than in the town I live in. The fellows have a fine streak of manliness in them about white women and children, and I heartily respect them for it."[203]

How to change this horrific oppression under which US women lived? The ballot was one necessary tool to overcome this "four-fold bondage" of woman by the "Church, State, Capital and Society," Stanton and Gage maintained.[204]

Denied a political role in their own nation, these two major theorists of the women's rights movement knew and wrote about the decision-making responsibilities of Haudenosaunee women. Stanton talked about how the clan mother had the responsibility for nominating and putting and holding in place the chief who represented her clan:

> The women were the great power among the clan, as everywhere else. They did not hesitate, when occasion required, "to knock off the horns," as it was technically called, from the head of a chief and send him back to the ranks of the warriors. The original nomination of the chiefs also always rested with the women.[205]

Gage wrote how authority was a balance of responsibilities, with everyone having a voice:

> Division of power between the sexes in this Indian republic was nearly equal. Although the principal chief of the confederacy was a man, descent ran through the female line.... The common interests of the confederacy were arranged in councils, each sex holding one of its own, although the women took the initiative in suggestion, orators of their own sex presenting their views to the council of men.[206]

When Matilda Joslyn Gage was adopted into the Wolf clan, Gage wrote that her adopted Mohawk sister told her that "this name would admit me to the Council of Matrons, where a vote would be taken, as to my having a voice in the Chieftainship."[207] How amazing this must have been to a woman who went to trial the same year for voting in a school board election! Considered for decision-making in her adopted nation, she was arrested in her own nation for voting.

The terrible irony, of course, is that at the same time the suffragists took vision from Indigenous women, their churches and government were systematically attempting to destroy the position these Native women held in their balanced societies. Through violent means and forced assimilation, the goal was to destroy the sovereign authority of the Native nations, and the sovereign authority of the women of these nations.

Sovereign women in a sovereign nation. The phrase resonates with me now. These are women who play a major role in the decolonization political awakening as Native nations reclaim their natural sovereignty, while they reassert their sovereignty as women in their nations. Once again, they will have control of their bodies, and the safety of knowing they will not be violated by those who are closest to them, as well as strangers. In the rare event that it happens, they know that their brothers will have their backs. They will never lose their children. They will have economic independence and authority, along with a political voice.

These sovereign women in sovereign nations before colonization had more rights and a higher position than women have under US law and society today, where one out of three of us will suffer violence, we make two-thirds of what men make in wages, we are underrepresented in every area of government, and we don't have equal rights guaranteed in the Constitution. As Native nations have maintained or are reclaiming sovereignty, the position of women remains enviable. The degree to which they have resisted forced assimilation and attempts to bring their nations completely under US law is the degree to which Native women continue to live in a society that practices equality. The model of sovereign women in sovereign nations remains a vision toward which to strive for US women still today.

The rich literature Indigenous women have developed since the 1960s, as their voices are increasingly finding print, is fueling the re-indigenizing process and shaping the direction, as discussed in the introduction to part II of this book. There are far too many to mention, but randomly pulling off my shelves, I find, for example:

Barbara A. Mann. *Iroquoian Women: The Gantowisas*. New York: Peter Lang, 2000.

Carolyn Dunn and Carol Comfort, eds. *Through the Eye of the Deer: An Anthology of Native American Women Writers*. San Francisco: Aunt Lute Books, 1999.

Yolanda Broyles-Gonzalez. *Re-Emerging Native Women of the Americas.* Dubuque, IA: Kendall/Hunt Publishing, 2001.

LeAnne Howe, *Shell Shaker.* San Francisco: Aunt Lute Books, 2001.

Susan Hazen-Hammond. *Spider Woman's Web: Traditional Native American Tales about Women's Power.* New York: Perigee, 1999.

Rebecca Kugel and Lucy Eldersveld Murphy, *Native Women's History in Eastern North America before 1900.* Lincoln: University of Nebraska Press, 2007. (An anthology of Native and non-Native authors.)

Marilou Awiakta. *Selu: Seeking the Corn-Mother's Wisdom.* Golden, CO: Fulcrum Publishing, 1993.

Carol Cornelius. *Iroquois Corn in a Culture-Based Curriculum: A Framework for Respectfully Teaching about Cultures.* Albany: State University of New York Press, 1999.

Winona LaDuke. *All Our Relations: Native Struggles for Land and Life.* Cambridge, MA: South End Press, 2008.

Patricia Monture-Angus. *Thunder in My Soul: A Mohawk Woman Speaks.* Halifax: Fernwood Publishing, 1995.

Andrea Smith. *Conquest: Sexual Violence and American Indian Genocide.* Cambridge, MA: South End Press, 2005.

Wilma Mankiller. *Every Day Is a Good Day: Reflections by Contemporary Indigenous Women.* Golden, CO: Fulcrum Publishing, 2004.

Joy Harjo and Gloria Bird. *Reinventing the Enemy's Language: Contemporary Native Women's Writings of North America.* New York: W. W. Norton & Company Inc., 1997.

Janet Sillman (as told to). *Enough Is Enough: Aboriginal Women Speak Out.* Toronto: The Women's Press, 1987.

Kim Anderson. *A Recognition of Being: Reconstructing Native Womanhood.* Toronto: Second Story Press, 2000.

Karen L. Kilcup, ed. *Native American Women's Writing, 1800–1924.* Oxford: Blackwell Publishers Ltd., 2000.

Laura F. Klein and Lillian A. Ackerman. *Women and Power in Native North America.* Norman: University of Oklahoma Press, 1995.

Section 4: The Impact of Indians on the Youth Movement of the 1960s

Ain Haas and Stephen M. Sachs

A major turning point in the evolution of Americans' attitudes toward Indians came in the 1960s, in connection with the youthful counterculture that developed in opposition to the prevailing order. The civil rights movement of the late 1950s and early 1960s, which sought to end discrimination against African Americans, had attracted a large number of white students and religious activists to its protest marches, voter registration drives, acts of civil disobedience, mass demonstrations, and so forth, and provided a model for mobilizing public opinion for other reforms. The growing opposition to the military draft and American involvement in the Vietnam War inspired the use of similar tactics by members of the postwar "baby boom" generation. Their great numbers, high education, and generally affluent upbringing added to their sense of efficacy and interest in new experiences, meaningful occupations, and alternative lifestyles. Contributing to the antiauthoritarian mood and criticism of the hypocrisy of "the establishment" was a widespread feeling that the pursuit of materialistic goals through monotonous jobs in bureaucratic work organizations was ultimately unfulfilling and even harmful to one's physical and mental health. For many in this nonconformist or countercultural movement, American Indians came to symbolize resistance to the dehumanizing "military-industrial complex" and offered a model worthy of emulation.

While learning about Indians in this context was not the original stimulus for the counterculture's interest in an alternative set of values, it was a significant factor in reinforcing their commitment to seeking a new way of life. Realizing that traditional Indian societies could be seen as exemplifying the core principles of the new counterculture's vision of a better way made the youth movement's goals seem more realistic and attainable. This can be seen in Gary

Snyder's realization that the lifestyle "based on community and comradeship, personal relations and responsibilities rather than abstract centralized government, taxes, propaganda, and law" had been tried before. He exhorted:

> Look at the lives of S. African Bushmen, Micronesian navigators, the Indians of California.... We have almost unintentionally linked ourselves to a transmission of values, a potential social order, and techniques of enlightenment, surviving from pre-historic times.[208]

As information about Indians was more accessible to members of the new American counterculture than material about other exemplars of the alternative lifestyle being sought, Indian influences became especially important in shaping the new rebels' views.

The focal point of the youth movement of the 1960s was in the Haight-Ashbury district of San Francisco, where large numbers of dropouts from conventional society and seekers of a new way congregated. The "hippies" who emerged there adopted many Indian elements in their appearance (e.g., fringed buckskin jackets, headbands, braids, and beaded necklaces). They often pointed to American Indians as living in exemplary harmony with nature, using appropriate and sustainable technology, forming an egalitarian tribal community that promoted redistribution of wealth and participatory decision-making, and allowing individuals to pursue highly personal forms of spiritual enlightenment through hallucinatory experiences (vision quests).

Although most of the hippies had only a superficial knowledge of Indian ways, many of them read books about Indians (a sizable sample of which are listed in the introduction to part II of this book), while their interest directly contributed to the proliferation of publications about Indians. Some counterculture youth also visited reservations, reached out to urban Indians to learn more, or took part in gatherings and teaching sessions with Indian leaders.

The hippies derived their name and many of their ideas from the previous generation's countercultural wave of "hipsters" or "the Beat Generation," which had originally been centered in New York City. Among the most influential intellectuals of this precursor movement was the novelist Ken Kesey, author of *One Flew over the Cuckoo's Nest*,[209] which was later made into an Oscar-winning film.[210] An important character in the novel—the only one who escapes from the oppressive authoritarian regime of a mental hospital—is the Indian narrator, who longs to see the salmon-fishing platforms that his people have erected near a hydroelectric dam in defiance of a power company's claims to private ownership of the riverbanks and the government's efforts to enforce such claims.

Sherry L. Smith[211] notes that Kesey's upbringing in Oregon gave him some familiarity with the history of local Indians' treaty-based claims of the right of access to their traditional fishing spots. Smith also notes that it would be hard to overstate Kesey's contribution as a bridge between the Beats and the hippies, and credits him with being "the first of his generation to turn to Indianness as inspiration for social criticism, political action, and cultural release." His experimentation with the drug LSD and membership in the group of traveling bohemians known as the Merry Pranksters also provided a model for both the psychedelic drug trips and disruptive happenings in which hippies engaged.

Among the readers who had been deeply moved by Kesey's novel was Stewart Brand, who was working at the time as a photographer on the Warm Springs Reservation in Oregon before joining the Merry Pranksters. He was inspired to visit other reservations for several years, to take more photos of contemporary Indians. For a tour of college campuses and community theaters, he prepared a multimedia show featuring photographic slides, film clips, audiotapes, and live performances called "America Needs Indians," which was meant to make audiences realize that Indians were still around and could teach the rest of America valuable lessons. This show became one of the highlights of the Trips Festival in San Francisco in January 1966, which Brand helped to organize and which also featured Ken Kesey and the Merry Pranksters.[212] As a result, interest in Indians became an integral part of the hippie subculture. Such interest also spread to other branches of the youth movement, such as the political activists who pointed to Indians as symbols of resistance to American militarism, genocide, and the draft.

Brand credited his Indian wife with helping to inspire his interest in the Earth as a harmonious whole. In his lectures, he raised the question of why the space program was not publicizing photographs of the whole planet from space, which inspired a retired military officer and NASA security specialist who attended one of Brand's lectures to take up this particular cause and thereby accelerate NASA's production and release of such photos.[213] The publication of such photos may in turn have given a boost to the emerging environmental movement, which clearly was accelerated by interest in Indians and their relation to nature as discussed below.

Brand used such a photo for the cover and even the basic concept of his next project, the *Whole Earth Catalog*, first published in 1968,[214] which provided a mail-order service to the countercultural communes that emerged in the 1960s. These sprang up particularly after Haight-Ashbury became overcrowded during the so-called Summer of Love in 1967, which drew some 100,000 new arrivals, as well as unwanted attention from tourists, narcotics dealers, and law enforcement officers. Derived from Brand's earlier traveling truck store for communards, the catalog became a best-selling publication, not just for the products but also for the practical advice and book reviews it provided. Along with tips on windmills and other inventions from the Old World, many things from Indian cultures were promoted. There was information on Indian tipis, footwear, crafts, survival arts, medicine, and religion.[215] Brand's publication was the only catalog ever to receive a National Book Award.

Another central figure in the hippie movement who emphasized the importance of learning about and emulating Indians was the poet Gary Snyder—his impact is also noted in the environmental section of this chapter below. Presiding over the event known as the 1967 San Francisco Be-in, he was characterized as one of the "most respected voices in the Beat-Hippie-Psychedelic movement" in the February 1967 issue of San Francisco's underground newspaper, *The Oracle*. That issue featured a lengthy article with Snyder's reflections on the importance of learning about the Indians' technology, family and tribal organizations, vision quests, rituals, mythologies, and deities, in the search for a better way to live. Some 125,000 copies of this issue were eventually printed.[216]

The next issue of *The Oracle* was devoted entirely to Indians. As preparation for the follow-up, the newspaper sent a group of artists and writers to visit the Hopi reservation in Arizona. The Hopi were of particular interest to the San Francisco hippies, probably because many of the latter had read the *Book of the Hopi* by Frank Waters. The tribe's pacifism, spirituality, and harmonious relationship with its environment were most appealing. The hippies of San Francisco aspired to follow a Hopi model of organization in setting up a community center called the "Kiva" (after the Hopi word for their underground ceremonial centers). In San Francisco, the Kiva was planned as a building that would be a place of instruction, art, and the development of self-supporting rural communes. The twelve men leading the organizing effort were known as the Kiva's "tribal council."[217]

More informed about Indian ways than most of the hippies in this new community, Snyder could draw on a long experience of observing and studying Native Americans. He had grown up on a dairy farm in the state of Washington where he came into contact with Salish and Wishram fishermen, and was impressed by the Indians' knowledge of animals' habits and low-impact technology. As a youth, he also noticed the devastation that mechanized logging was doing to the local environment. His first visit to a reservation came at Warm Springs as a student in 1949, and he planned to study anthropology in Indiana University's graduate program. Instead he decided to explore East Asians' religions, since Indians tended to be rather secretive about their beliefs and rituals, which was not surprising in the context of discouragement of traditional religions by missionaries and government officials. Snyder's book of poems, *Turtle Island,* published in 1974 and based on an Indian name for the North American continent, won the Pulitzer Prize and led to an increase in his readership and influence far beyond San Francisco.[218]

Another noteworthy figure in the San Francisco counterculture was Peter Coyote (originally Cohon), one of the council members of the San Francisco Kiva and a founding member of the Diggers, later called the Free City Collective, which was a theater collective that had split off from the San Francisco Mime Troupe in order to discard a hierarchical administrative structure, and to stage theatrical events on the street and in other improvised settings. It was guerrilla theater for the purpose of making people think critically about the existing system, and to demonstrate how Indigenous-style generosity and reciprocity, rather than money, could be the basis of an economy that could support the Haight-Ashbury community.

The collective organized giveaway events and opened three stores beginning in December 1966, where people could obtain food, clothing, and even money for free. From a nearby commune, they brought apples and other foods to distribute for free. Even theft was a source of goods to be redistributed. The name of the group originally came from the English Diggers of the seventeenth century who had resisted the enclosure (privatization) of common lands after the overthrow of the monarchy in 1649. But it also evoked images of hipsters enjoying or "digging" the countercultural scene, as well as California's Indians who dug for wild roots and lived without money, private property, or destruction of the environment.[219]

The Diggers promoted the slogans of "Do your own thing" and "It's free because it's yours" in order to encourage "members of the Haight-Ashbury community to liberate themselves by claiming and enacting, rather than asking for, their freedoms."[220] The goal was to create an anarchist community that circumvented the money system, the perceived source of American society's "most pernicious evils."[221] Their thinking was that the existing system would simply collapse if enough people refused to follow the rules and began acting as if they were free.

In his memoirs, *Sleeping Where I Fall,*[222] Coyote emphasized the importance of the Diggers' spontaneous and anonymous tactics, which made it impossible for law enforcement to infiltrate the group and make arrests, in contrast to what happened to the yippies (Youth International Party), who courted media attention with their antics.[223] The Diggers joined the dispersal of hippies from Haight-Ashbury in 1968, and then went on to other things. But their style of guerilla theater continues to be emulated by others seeking social change.

Coyote's characterization of the Diggers' approach is reminiscent of many Indian societies' openness to individual initiative: "If you have a fantasy, take responsibility for it and actualize it, build or imply a society around it. And if it's nice, people will join you."[224] When he subsequently went to live in an anarchic commune in 1969 "where people could be and do what they wanted," Coyote emerged as an informal leader there, and felt the need to seek guidance for his new role. In addition to interacting with the local Karuks, Yuroks, and Hoopas, he went on a road trip to the Southwest to visit communes in New Mexico and the nearby Hopi reservation.

There his Indian hosts avoided giving him direct advice, but invited him to stay with them for several days. The experience had a profound effect on him, as reflected in his writing:

> I realize that the most important gift we received [w]as the opportunity to witness and participate in an ancient, ordered spiritual life.... We were afforded a glimpse into a self-sufficient system that had taken thousands of years to develop. The lightness of their personal lives, the absence of the demands they made on the environment and each other was chastening and elevating.[225]

Hundreds of counterculture communes sprouted in rural areas beginning in the 1960s, with considerable Native American inspiration. A major impulse of most communards was to create close, supportive interpersonal communities that they envisioned had been the core of tribal communities.[226] Many participants sought a return "to the tribal position of the American Indian or the more satisfying life of a more closely knit extended family—a situation where adults and children can live more intimately and humanely in a cohesive, face-to-face primary group."[227]

Timothy Miller noted several other counterculture identifications with their view of Indians:

> The lure of the countryside also meshed well with counter-cultural fascination with Native Americans, who were frequently seen as embodying a profound nature wisdom long lost to nonnative peoples....
>
> The Indian connection would continue through the 1960s communal era; good relationships with local Indian tribes were developed at several communes...and even absent a direct local Indian connection, communards in many places lived in tepees, wore loincloths while hoeing their crops, and came together for peyote rituals....
>
> [T]he ideal of open land, enunciated at several of the earliest post-1960 communes, was powerful and was embraced (at least intermittently) at hundreds of communes.[228]

The idea of collective living for most of the post-1960s communards also embraced a tribal perspective that rejected the idea of private ownership of land. Pam Hanna, who had been a member of several communes, writes,

> Parceling up Mother Earth is a foreign and ludicrous concept to so many Indians, which is perhaps why hippies and Indians usually got along well.[229]

Miller also notes how the new communards applied their new-found knowledge of Indian ways to solve practical problems in areas like health care. This was done through adoption of some traditional healing practices from Indians. At Wheeler's Ranch in California, for example:

> With professional medical treatment unavailable, people turned to folk and Indian remedies. Studying Miwok tribal customs brought the ranch another wonderful way to cure winter ailments. A sweat lodge was built out of bent branches covered with plastic.[230]

In one of the earliest books about the 1960s communes, *The Alternative: Communal Life in New America* published in 1970, William Hedgepeth draws attention to the appeal of still another aspect of Indian tradition: consensual decision-making. He notes communal societies that were an offshoot of the hippie movement "insist on arriving at all policy decisions through complete, unanimous decisions, Indian-style."[231]

Among the best-known of the southwestern communes was New Buffalo, near the Taos Pueblo in New Mexico. Characterized by Lois Rudnick as "the archetypal hippie commune," its members "found inspiration primarily in Native American practices." The communards came to the area with some misguided notions about the local Native lifestyle but adapted well to the mentoring the Natives offered.

For example, the newcomers' tipis were soon abandoned in favor of the sturdier and cooler adobe houses that the local Indians showed them how to build, and they also followed the Natives' example in their choices of crops and construction of a kiva. The commune continued as such into the 1980s, eventually evolving into "the home base of the Sustainable Native Agricultural Center, a nonprofit group dedicated to preserving native seeds, and then a bed and breakfast [operation] designed to attract tourists interested in Taos' countercultural past."[232]

Meanwhile, numerous counterculture people, and by the 1970s a good many more mainstream people, began seeking Indian traditional teachers by going to Indian-led gatherings and supporting

Indian ceremonies. This helped the sale of books about Indians, which in turn brought more non-Indians to seek Indian teachings and to be actively involved with Native Americans. Among the better-known Indian spiritual leaders involved in this activity was Lakota Spiritual Leader ("medicine man") Wallace Black Elk, who felt it important to connect with whites for the renewal of the hoop of the world, as foretold by one of his teachers and spiritual, but not blood, grandfathers, Nick Black Elk, in *Black Elk Speaks*.[233] Thus, Wallace Black Elk often participated in Indian-led gatherings, including those of Sun Bear.[234]

Another Indian leader who worked with non-Indians was Northern California's Karuk medicine man Charlie Red Hawk Thom, who for many years led sweat lodges and journeys to Mount Shasta with non-Indians of the Earth Circle Association.[235] Southern Ute of Colorado grandmother Bertha Grove, her husband Vincent Grove, and her brother, Sun Dance chief Everett Birch, also worked with non-Indians, sometimes traveling to Michigan and other places for teaching gatherings.[236]

It is important to note that while much of the work with non-Indians has been genuine and well undertaken, there have been complaints that some teachings by certain Indians were not well done, or were not properly taken by the non-Indians involved. Much of this is a problem in mainstream American culture that has two aspects. One is a rush to attain things instantly, rather than taking the time necessary to achieve deep learnings over a long period of time through extended experience. It is a tendency likely partly resulting from watching television shows in which major problems are solved in thirty minutes or an hour. Thus, after just one weekend at an Indian gathering, some folks naively would go off and start leading sweat lodges, with no real understanding of what they were doing. The second aspect is the emphasis on money in American culture, which across many spiritual and religious traditions has become a perversion. As one Sufi teacher bemoaned at a public session, "Spirituality has become a growth industry."[237] This problem encompasses the rise of "plastic medicine men," which is something many Indians complain about.

A few non-Indians became so identified with Indigenous Americans that they took on Indian names. Among the better known was hippie spiritual leader John Pope, widely known as Rolling Thunder. Born in Oklahoma in 1916, he and his wife Spotted Fawn founded a commune on 262 acres just east of the town of Carlin, Nevada. Pope claimed to be an Indian medicine man, and became widely known through Doug Boyd's 1974 book, *Rolling Thunder.*[238]

Another was Iron Eyes Cody, who made a career of acting as an Indian, including starring in a 1971 TV commercial showing an Indian in a canoe crying about pollution. That single advertisement gave a big boost to the environmental movement discussed more fully below. Although he always denied it, Cody was of Italian heritage, according to a close relative; nevertheless he was a strong supporter of American Indian issues throughout his career.[239]

Although the relationship between Indians and countercultural types like the new communards was generally quite amicable and mutually appreciative,[240] there was always some inherent tension. The hippies tended to see what they wanted to see in the Natives' culture, not always being aware of or caring about the traditional context. For example, new "dope churches" modeled after the Native American Church sprang up for communal drug use when hippies realized that peyote was the only psychedelic substance that could be legally used. However, this was more of a hedonistic recreational activity rather than one of several pathways in a serious pursuit of spiritual insights, guided by elders, as it is among the Indians.[241]

A connection also developed between rock music and Indians; this association began in relation to the counterculture drug involvement. Concerning the music group The Doors, Miriam Hahn states:

> [Jim] Morrison, known to other members of the Doors as the "electric shaman" ... evokes another highly romanticized

image of the Native—that of the mystic healer or shaman who takes hallucinogenic drugs in order to achieve spiritual awakening. For hippies who were experimenting with peyote, LSD, mushrooms, marijuana, and other psychoactive stimulants, the Native American mystic was a convenient mascot, one who lent an imagined sense of ancient cultural legitimacy to the practice of getting high and set a seemingly irrefutable precedent for the use of drugs as conduits to spiritual realms.[242]

The counterculture, including its mind-altering drug experimentation and practice, contributed to a change in American spirituality beyond Indigenous American ways. It also was an important source of the huge rise in interest, beyond the counterculture (and without interest in mind-altering substances), in Eastern religions, including Hinduism, Buddhism, and Sufism, and in other experiential and mystical spiritual paths as discussed in the part II introduction.

Besides having somewhat divergent views on the purpose, proper context, and recommended frequency of using mind-altering substances, the new counterculture and Indians differed on other points as well. While Indian societies often had a greater degree of sexual freedom in some respects, as illustrated by the institution of the berdache among the Plains tribes, where some males took on the gender identity and social status of females, and Indian women's equal rights with regard to initiating and terminating relationships, there were typically restrictions on intra-clan marriages, punishments for adultery, and requirements for coverings for the genital areas (even if women might have been traditionally topless in warmer climes), and there was no widespread encouragement of promiscuity.

Also, the antiwar activists who sought to publicize Native anti-draft martyrs had considerable trouble finding them. Indians had a tendency to respect warriors and veterans, regardless of their feelings about the military enterprise in Vietnam, while the youth movement tended to disparage anyone who participated in the war or wore a military uniform. Hippies tended to ignore or downplay the conflict between tribalism and self-indulgence, while Indians were traditionally more inclined to act for the good of the group rather than to exercise total individual freedom.[243] The counter-cultural movement was especially interested in Indian societies as they were before traditions had been disrupted by contact with or subjugation by European settlers, but Indians had to worry about adapting to current conditions and dealing with poverty, abrogation of treaty rights, and discrimination.

The counterculture tended to stereotype Indians in the search for symbols and mascots for its causes, in ways that implied that Indians were intractable opponents of modernity or destined to remain marginal members of American society. Yet there was something new in their approach: the stereotypes were predominantly positive, from the perspective of the non-Indians promulgating them. This helps explain why there was a sudden shift in Hollywood films' portrayal of Indians after the 1960s as discussed in the introduction to part II. They were no longer portrayed as threats to pioneers or soldiers, but as victims of injustice and as protagonists performing heroic deeds.

Indians' protests in the 1960s and '70s also changed press coverage of them and impacted public opinion. Their acts of rebellion in this period escalated from defiance of fishing bans to more militant actions. These included the occupation of the closed prison at Alcatraz Island in the San Francisco Bay in 1969–71, the seizure of the offices of the Bureau of Indian Affairs in Washington, DC, in 1972 after a nationwide procession called the Trail of Broken Treaties, and the American Indian Movement's takeover of Wounded Knee on the Pine Ridge Reservation in South Dakota in 1973.

In response, the press coverage no longer emphasized the quaintness of traditionalist Indians or the escapades of non-Indian celebrities supporting them, but focused on Indians' grievances and the historical context. Non-Indians became important providers of support services and even joined the ranks of the protesters, while respecting the Indian rebels' wishes to retain leadership of such events. As Sherry L. Smith states in *Hippies, Indians, and the Fight for Red Power*:

> Reporters appeared to accept the counterculture image of Indianness, neither ridiculing nor dismissing it. Consequently, the celebration of Indian ways continued to seep into the national consciousness, finding receptive audiences not only among the liberal, progressive churches that had joined forces with the tribes,...but also among people who had never previously given Indians a thought.[244]

As a result, Indians' protest actions gained traction in an unprecedented way.[245] Although the Alcatraz occupation did not end with the government's recognition of Indians' efforts to reclaim the island, there were subsequent land transfers elsewhere to make possible a pan-Indian university and an Indian cultural center, which had been among the primary goals of the Alcatraz takeover. After the Wounded Knee incident,

> The American Indian Movement, in particular, captured the interest and support of America's New Left and politically oriented counterculture. Along for the ride were many mainstream organizations. Even the president of the United States and at least some of his men were paying attention.[246]

The Nixon administration moved away from a plan to promote termination of the reservation system, and the Justice Department began to defend Indian treaty rights. Congress and the courts also "acquiesced to Indian demands for more power over their lives and resources," and the tribes whose reservations had been terminated began to get some relief of their hardships.[247]

The move away from termination actually began with the Kennedy administration's not continuing to carry out the termination policy begun under the Eisenhower administration, before the hippie phenomenon in San Francisco. The civil rights movement, the growth and increased effectiveness of Indian organizations, and their adept leadership were initially the most important factors.[248] The War on Poverty under the Johnson administration, which included an American Indian set of poverty programs, further reflected and expanded Indians' direct influence on US Indian policy.[249] The next step came with the Nixon administration's formally switching from the policy of termination to self-determination. By that time the counterculture was having more influence, which combined with the increased efforts of Indian leaders and activists, as well as the greater openness in the Nixon administration, to further advance American Indian rights and interests.

In short, the counterculture's interest in Indians, even if it was often superficial and misguided, played an important role in helping to change the political climate in ways that brought more respect, understanding, legal victories, and other gains for the Indians. As a consequence, the assimilationist pressure let up, and more Americans than ever before have been willing to let Indians keep some semblance of their sovereignty and traditions. This new-found tolerance is an extension of what the European settlers had been learning from the Indians all along, to respect diversity and others' personal freedom. Moreover, the counterculture interest in Indians contributed significantly to the growth of the environmental movement, which Indians influenced in major ways, as discussed in the next section.

Section 5: The Impact of Indians on the Environmental Movement: The Ecological Indian

Walter S. Robinson and Stephen M. Sachs

Ingrained in the American mind is the motif of the "ecological Indian," which stands as an icon of the environmental movement.

By some measure it is a stereotype emerging out of Eurocentric imagination: part of a complex sociopolitical history and ethno-psychology of Western thought. On the other hand it is not all together divorced from the ecological wisdom to be found in American Indian philosophies. Moreover, because it is a reflection stemming from early contact of Europeans with Indians, the image became popularized in a television advertisement of an Indian in a canoe crying at the pollution in the water.[250] As the impact of the environmental movement grew in a changing US culture, which included a generally increasingly favorable picture of Indians, the image of the environmental Indian was reinforced in the 1995 animated epic musical romantic-drama film *Pocahontas*.[251] Meanwhile the image of the ecological Indian has permeated US environmental education.[252]

Two Western Views of Indians and the Environmental Crisis

When the first modern Europeans invaded what they would come to call "America," they carried with them a philosophy that is the root of the contemporary environmental crisis. Those they called Indians were seen as "other," in one widespread view, and were stereotyped as bloodthirsty savages living in the wild. This wilderness and the people dwelling therein were conceived of as being in need of subduing and domesticating. Thomas Hobbes, as is discussed in chapter 3, declared that man living in a state of nature is in a state of war, each against all others; that civil society was the way out of this most malevolent condition. The historical backdrop of this belief is a Judeo-Christian notion of nature's being fallen and under the dominion of the Devil. The need to subdue the land and to civilize people was akin to a war against evil. The old pagan religions, including the many forms of American Indian spirituality, were feared to be devil worship. Thus for God's sake the Indians needed either to be exterminated or civilized and the land domesticated according to civil norms.

Antithetical to this Hobbesian paradigm and much of the Western philosophical tradition is the position of Jean-Jacques Rousseau, discussed in chapter 3. For him the American Indian was a "noble savage" living more or less at peace in a state of nature. Thus he disagreed with Hobbes that man in nature was in a state of war—in truth it is civilization that is more warlike; humanity was better off before the advent of civilization. The mythos of the ecological Indian in Eurocentric imagination is grounded in the Rousseauian paradigm, though in many instances the source was from others than Rousseau, as discussed at length above.

Thoreau: A Founder of the Environmental Movement

Euro-American perspectives of Indians have historically involved a dialectic tension between Hobbesian and Rousseauian paradigms. Henry David Thoreau, whose writings are foundational to American environmentalists, was significantly influenced by Rousseau, as well as by what he learned from Indians themselves and others who knew them, or were directly or indirectly influenced by them.[253] There are more than 1,900 references in Thoreau's writings to Indians in ways that reflect the "noble savage" thesis. In his journal Thoreau writes:

The charm of the Indian to me is that he stands free and unconstrained in nature—is her inhabitant—and not her guest—and wears her easily and gracefully.[254]

He then goes on to write critical assertions of "civilized man" in a fashion congruent with Rousseau's critique of civilization. Indeed throughout his writings Thoreau is critical of civil norms. In his essay "Life without Principle," he writes:

If a man walk in the woods for love of them half of each day, he is in danger of being regarded as a loafer; but if he spends his whole day as a speculator, shearing off those woods and making earth bald before her time, he is esteemed an industrious and enterprising citizen. As if a town had no interest in its forests but to cut them down.[255] ... Cold and hunger seem more friendly to my nature than those methods which [civilized] men have adopted and advice to ward then off.[256]

The word "citizen" means to be of civilization, whereas the root meaning of "civilization" is "being of the city." Both Rousseau and Thoreau use the word "savage" in contradiction to civilization. Thoreau repeatedly uses the term "savage" in reference to Indians in a manner consistent with its root meaning and not in accord with a Hobbesian prejudice. He points out in *The Maine Woods* that the etymology of "savage" is from the Latin "sylva," which means "woods," whereas those who live in the woods were called "selvaggia," from which we derive the Old French "salvage" and the Middle English "sauvage."[257]

As a student at Harvard, Thoreau wrote a paper for a class on the subject of standards for judging civilization, in which he argued a position consistent with Rousseau's opinion that civilization is more harmful than not. Moreover Thoreau argued that the arts of civil life place man at odds with the natural world. He wrote:

> The justice of a nation's claim to be regarded as civilized seems to depend, mainly upon the degree in which Art has triumphed over Nature. The culture implied by the term Civilization is the influence of Art, not Nature on man.[258]

The word "art" is related to being artificial, which is to be made by human activity in contradiction to organic nature; the latter is not made but grows spontaneously by virtue of a self-generative ecology. The savage Indian is imagined by Thoreau as living in an eco-centered harmony with what is natural. In his journal he writes:

> The pine stands in the woods like an Indian—untamed—with fantastic wildness about it ever in the clearing.[259] ... The best [civilized] poets, after all, exhibit only a tame and civil side of nature—they have not seen the west [savage] side

of any mountain. Day and night—mountain and wood are visible from the wilderness as well as the village—they have their primeval aspects—sterner savager—than any poet has sung.[260] ... If we could get a clear report from the Indian it would be different—for he is more conversant with pure nature. We should do him more justice and understand better why he will not exchange his savageness for civilization.[261]

The Changing Mainstream West and the Indigenous

However, Thoreau's opinion was not shared by most Euro-Americans of his historical period. The Hobbesian view dominated the nineteenth century, rationalizing the "march of progress" and "manifest destiny" with its genocidal and ecocidal consequence. The twentieth century began a paradigm shift to the Rousseauian view, arising with ecology and the environmental movement. For example, the image of Iron Eyes Cody in a pro-environmental television commercial in the role of an ecological Indian shedding a single tear in response to pollution became iconographic to the popular culture.[262] There is also the famous speech of Chief Sealth, which alluded to Native American ecological wisdom.

Chief Sealth, for whom the city of Seattle was named, was an elder of the Duwamish. In 1854 he gave a speech on the eve of his people's being moved from their ancestral lands. He spoke in his native language, which was translated into English. This was witnessed by a physician named Henry Smith, who took notes of it and would later write it out, publishing it in the *Seattle Star* in 1887.

In 1970 Ted Perry wrote a revision for a documentary film on ecological concerns. Perry made it clear after the fact that his revision of the Chief Sealth speech was fictional, and not to be taken as historical. Other versions based more on Perry's have emerged in popular culture, creating a mythos around Chief Sealth. A question arises as to what extent this mythos is true to authentic Indian philosophy? It is reasonable to assume that the original version as recorded by Smith is true to the intended meaning of Sealth.

Moreover, it is congruent with Indigenous perspective, as may be known though an inventory of sources originating from other Native Americans.

In the original speech Sealth is cited as saying, "The ashes of our ancestors are sacred and their resting place is hallowed ground." He goes on to say, "Our religion is the tradition of our ancestor," which he tells us comes to the people from the Great Spirit though dreams and visions.[263] The term "Great Spirit" is often taken as a synonym for "God"; however, one needs to be careful in this interpretation as Indigenous spirituality differs significantly from monotheism. Sealth made clear that there is a difference, saying, "Your [white] God is not our [Indian] God! Your God loves your people and hates mine."[264]

The white God steeped in a then widely popular version of Judeo-Christian tradition is one that is a transcendental creator deity beyond the world, outside of time and space. In this view, human beings were seen as separate from nature. Moreover, holders of this perspective interpreted the Bible as saying that human beings had "dominion" over nature,[265] and as Locke expressed in the *Second Treatise on Government*, a responsibility to develop the resources of nature for human use. Whereas the Indian God belongs to a pantheistic animism, in which creation is an ongoing process in cyclical time and sacred space.

Vine Deloria Jr., in his book *God Is Red,* draws major distinctions between monotheism and American Indian religions. Most important for the discourse on environmental concerns is the notion of sacred geography. In words attributed to Sealth, "Every part of this soil is sacred . . . . Every hillside, every valley, every plain and grove,"[266] because this world is sacred, it must be treated with reverence and respect. The term "Mother Earth" is often used to denote the sacredness of the natural world. This motif is archetypal in scope.

The idea of the Earth as mother and the sky as father can be found cross-culturally not only among hundreds of American Indian tribes but also among other indigenous people, such as the

Polynesians, and in ancient China, and even in the old pagan religions of Europe.[267] In the *Theogony* of Hesiod we read that Mother
Earth gives birth to the world and is the ancestor of all the gods.
James Lovelock uses the name of the Greek earth goddess Gaia
to name his theory of the biosphere's ecological wholeness. Native
American spirituality is akin to the oldest, most widespread religions, whereas monotheism is a much more recent development, a
radical divergence from its predecessors.

The oldest religions were/are nature-based, whereby there is
no separation between the spiritual and the material; they are two
aspects of a unity. The circle or Sacred Hoop is a metaphor for this
unity. Of this, Black Elk said:

> You have noticed that everything an Indian does is in a cir-
> cle, and that is because the Power of the World always works
> in circles, and everything tries to be round.... Birds make
> their nest in circles for theirs is the same religion as ours.[268]

In other words, indigenous religions are shared by all nature, by
all life. Some nineteenth-century and later popular interpretations
of monotheistic religions hold that religion is made for man only by
some supernatural agent. The difference here is that the former is
eco-centric and the latter anthropocentric.

Vine Deloria Jr. points out that monotheism has a concept of
time which is linear, quite different from the cyclical notion of time
among Indians. In Hebrew-based mythos there is an absolute beginning of time and an end—an alpha and an omega. Thus we have an
apocalyptic obsession among some Christians with the end-times.
According to the monotheistic creation story, sometime after the
beginning and early on is the "Fall," by which sin enters the world
so that people became corrupted and became capable of relating
to nature in an evil way. In this view, salvation is attained, in part,
by escape from and/or conquest of the natural world through the
help of supernatural agency. This kind of belief is an anti-organic
nature phobia, and civilization is built on this. A metaphor for this

mind-set is a broken circle, of which ecologist Barry Commoner asserts results in an environmental crisis:

> Human beings have broken out of the circle of life, driven not by biological need but by social organization which they have devised to "conquer nature."[269]

The Historical Roots of the Ecological Crisis

In 1969 Lynn White published a paper *The Historical Roots of Our Ecologic Crisis*. In it he writes that the "victory of Christianity over paganism was the greatest psychic revolution in the history of our [Western] culture."[270] The root meaning of the word "pagan" is related to those who dwell in the countryside outside of the cities. Christianity in Europe became the dominant religion of the cities, which is to say of civilization. The pagans were akin to the savages living within and in accord to the natural world. The Christian motif of the Devil is based in part on Pan and Robin Goodfellow (also known as Puck), who lives wild in the forest and is said to be the god of the witches. In the same historical period that Europeans were invading America and committing genocide on Indians and ecocide on the land, much of the same was happening in Europe against paganism, whereby the Inquisition committed mass murder of hundreds of thousands of people (mostly women) in the witch burnings.

The time of the witch burnings was a historical antecedent to the rise of modern science, technology, and industrialization—so it is not surprising that Francis Bacon used metaphors related to the Inquisition for the new science, saying that Mother Nature will be put on the rack to torture her for her secrets.

Modern science is not a break from the religious past, but is continuous with the same underlying attitudes. However, it is important to note that Western science has been shifting toward a more Indigenous way of seeing since at least the beginning of the twentieth century, as discussed in the introduction to part II of this book.

In some of the more popular English translations of the biblical creation story, we read:

Let us make man in our image, after our likeness. And let them have dominion over the fish of the sea and the birds of the heavens and the livestock and over the earth and over every creeping thing that creeps on the earth.[271]

And as this version of the story goes, once man was created, God says to him:

Be fruitful and multiply and fill the earth and subdue it and have dominion over the fish of the sea and the birds of the heavens and over every living thing that moves on the earth."[272]

This mythos thus implies that nonhuman life was created for human use, and that humanity is commanded by divine authority to have dominion over it. Lynn White gives what seems like commentary on such biblical assertions:

Christianity is the most anthropocentric religion the world has seen.... In [pre-Christian pagan] Antiquity every tree, every spring, every hill had its own genius, its guardian spirit.... By destroying pagan animism, Christianity made it possible to exploit nature in a mood of indifference to the feelings of natural objects.[273]

White does find one important voice with an Indigenous view of nature in Christian history, one that in the early twenty-first century would return to blend with Indigenous thinking:

Possibly we should ponder the greatest radical in Christian history since Christ: Saint Francis of Assisi. The prime miracle of Saint Francis is the fact that he did not end at the stake, as many of his left-wing followers did. He was so clearly heretical that a General of the Franciscan Order, Saint Bonaventura, a great and perceptive Christian, tried to suppress the early accounts of Franciscanism. The key to an understanding of Francis is his belief in the virtue of humility—not merely for the individual but for man as a species. Francis tried to depose man from his monarchy over creation and set up a democracy of all God's creatures. With him the ant is no longer simply a homily for the lazy, flames a sign of the thrust of the soul toward union with God; now they are Brother Ant and Sister Fire, praising the Creator in their own ways as Brother Man does in his.[274]

The Impact of Black Elk and Other Indigenous Voices

In the last quarter of the twentieth century, rising environmental crises combined with changes underway in Western culture, and particularly in the United States, as discussed in the introduction to part II below, a door opened to movement toward returning to Indigenous thinking. American Indians considerably contributed to this shift, both through current voices and increasingly popular earlier literature, such as *Black Elk Speaks*.

Black Elk's Lakota religion is an egalitarian eco-spirituality shared in partnership with the four-legged, the fish of the sea, the birds of the sky, and the things that creep on the earth, as well as the vegetation, the rocks, the rivers and mountains, and the whole of the natural world. Lakota has this expression "Mitakuye Oyas'in," meaning "all my relations," which is to say that all living beings are related. This parallels the concept in ecology of the interconnections and interdependency of everything.

However, unlike scientific ecology, this is much more intimate, more akin to Deep Ecology. When Chief Sealth and others like him refer to ancestors, part of the meaning is human relations are in one's own family tree, but even more so, they are also related to all living beings from which those of us in the present moment are descendants. There is a personal relatedness in all this, in that animals, plants, and even minerals are seen as people. There is kinship with the Buffalo people who have their tribe, along with other such people as the Elk tribe, Beaver tribe, and so forth, including the varieties of plants species, fungi, and so forth.

Consistent with evolutionary biology, which recognizes the interrelated origins of all life, there is agreement with tribal wisdom that humans are a more recent arrival. A common anthropocentric interpretation of this in the West interprets this to mean that humans are superior. But in the eco-centric perspective there is no superior or inferior, just differences, all expressing the beauty of diversity. In any case because humans have the least experience as a species and are so young in geological time, the animals and plants that have been around longer help their younger relatives.

This web of interdependent existence stands as an interpersonal community. In some of the Algonquian languages the very grammar is embedded with terms of personal relations with phenomena of the natural world. In most if not all Indigenous cosmologies there are personal relations with ecology. The synergy of all relationships is the Great Spirit. In Lakota the term is Wakan Tanka; in Algonquian languages like Ojibwe, Ottawa, and Potawatomi, the term is Gitche Manitou. Wakan and Manitou have the same basic meaning, which can be translated as "spirit," and also as "mystery." Tanka and Gitche both can mean "great" or "big." The root of the word "spirit" is from Latin "spiritus," which means "breath" as a life-giving energy. The same connotation applies to the Chinese word "Ch'i," which translates as bio-energy, and in Sanskrit there is the word "prana," which again means "breath" and" bio-energy." Then in Polynesia there is the word "mana," which once again means "life force energy." In Polynesian mythology deities are understood as personifications of mana. A similar belief exists among the Pueblo and Navajo with respect to the Kachinas.

The Advent of Modernity

Animism is rejected by the dominant mode of modern intellectualism. With the advent of modernity many religious ideas were challenged by intellectual elites. Hobbes was among these and is perhaps the first high-profile historically significant atheistic materialist. Drawing on the science of his day, he views the world as a machine made up of lifeless bits of matter, subject to fixed and blind laws that determine how things happen. This view overlaps with Cartesian metaphysics, at least with regard to what Descartes called "extended substance."

Descartes postulated a duality between mind or thinking substance and matter or extended substance, the latter being mechanical in nature, and the former capable of free will. This view is steeped in classical Platonism with its body/soul, matter/mind dualism. Here physicality is viewed as bad and that which is pure mind devoid of body is good. Augustine and other medieval theologians integrated Platonic dualism into Christian thought. Building on this historically given duality and adding the mechanics of modern science as descriptive of the physical world gives us the bases for Cartesian metaphysics. God still has a place in this story as the architect or engineer who designed and built the machine. So the universe is an artifact, just like the civilization which produced the mind-set for this kind of thinking. For Descartes only man has soul; animals, plants, and inanimate objects do not. There is no room in this view for Manitou, and as for God, he is an absentee landlord.

Hobbes rejects this duality and reduces everything to matter and mechanical laws. Thus there is no place for the spiritual. The only substance is matter, and mind is an epiphenomenon of brain activity. This view informs much of the modern mind-set and is the precursor to industrialization, which in turn contributes most significantly to the current environmental crisis. Lynn White writes that "modern Western science was cast in a matrix of Christian theology."

For the modern scientific man, God is out of the picture, or rendered not relevant to political and economic concerns. Just the same modernity emphasizes subduing and dominating the earth. This has been the case from the beginning of the modern era as seen in Hobbes. His political philosophy is one of domination and control. In this vein John Locke uses the language of "subduing and improving," feeding into the modern myth of progress as discussed in chapter 3. The modern concept of property is informed by Locke's definition that something becomes owned by removing it from a state of nature though labor.

From this perspective, nature is viewed as resources or commodities for economic profit. Like Hobbes, Locke sees civil society as a means to get out of a state of nature, and the end of civil law is to subdue and improve the natural world, reshaping it into the products of industry, that is to say, artifacts. The consequence of this is to live in an artificial environment removed from nature. The Indians were seen to be wasting valuable resources for not producing industry that would convert the stuff of nature into commodities. Indigenous culture, as discussed in chapter 1 of this book, did not have such an idea of property as understood by Locke, for nature was not an "it" but a "thou," with whom people may have a personal relation, and moreover this relationship was held to be sacred.

The Hobbesian and Rousseauian Views

Both the Hobbesian and Rousseauian views of aboriginal people are stereotypes forged out of Eurocentric imagination, projected onto others. Psychologically it tells us more about the European ethos than that of Indigenous people. The concept of nature and people living in nature is shaped by historical attitudes so deeply embedded in the cultural ethos as to be mostly subconscious and, therefore, seemingly self-evident. What is understood as "wild" is seen through a lens of social conditioning.

Indigenous people view the "wild" in a very different way. Of this, Lakota leader Luther Standing Bear said:

We did not think of the great open plains, the beautiful rolling hills, and winding streams with tangled brush, as "wild." Only to the white man was nature "a wilderness" and only to him was the land "infested" with "wild" animals and "savage" people.[275]

The word "wild" is a relational term in contrast to what is taken as being "tame." The Hobbesian concept of wild is a reaction to fear of nature. Rousseau seems less afraid of nature and more afraid of political tyranny. But either way both were projecting, seeing Indians through the lenses of their personal and cultural experiences. Indians were not solitary individuals, as Rousseau,[276] in some interpretations, and Thoreau seem to have imagined, but lived in tight-knit communities. Most lived in villages, some rather large, and most Indian tribes were agriculturally based.

American Indians also cultivated more different species of foodstuffs than any other people in the world. What they did not do in North America was domesticate animals—for meat Indians would hunt and fish. Europeans were nowhere nearly as sophisticated in plant cultivation as American Indians,[277] but they did advance in the domestication of animals. There is a significant psychosocial difference between cultivation and domestication. With cultivation there is working with nature to actualize that which is inherent in the plants.

Domestication is more in line with domination and control, which goes against the grain of what is natural; it is akin to the Hobbesian project, which aims to remove what it can out of the state of nature. Animals become livestock, and humans become citizens. The civil-minded people are politically indoctrinated in ways that separate people from their innate inclinations. This leads to civilized man having a nature phobia, so that what is natural is viewed as inferior, for some people even bad or sinful, and thus is in need of being changed. This is an anti-organic condition, like being psycho-spiritually castrated. From the point of view of such a crippled humanity, those not so inflicted may seem as wild, but for those not so injured, living in a state of nature is joyous and full of love. The tameness of nature for someone like Standing Bear reflects the serenity he felt being in harmony with the natural world. As he said:

> To us it [Nature] was tame. Earth was bountiful, and we are surrounded with the blessing of the Great Mystery.[278]

The Philosophy of Deep Ecology

What Standing Bear is expressing in common with other ecologically sensitive people is a philosophy of Deep Ecology. The phrase "deep ecology" was coined in 1973 by the Norwegian philosopher Arne Næss.[279] It has since become axiomatic to the environmental movement. The term "deep" is used in contradiction to "shallow"— the latter describes scientific ecology, which skims the surface of phenomena without the depth of feelings of aesthetics and love. If one is trapped in the paradigm of atheistic materialism, then the mind comprehends only the surface of life and not its depth. With atheistic materialism nature is mute and devoid of meaning. It is in the depth of being that one finds values and meaning; without such one falls into the paralysis of nihilism. With deep ecological sensitivity nature is not mute! She sings! The sound of birds, insects, frogs, the wind moving through rustling leaves, the sound of flowing water in a mountain stream and that of rhythmic surf—she speaks in an ancient language that communicates the harmony of the biosphere.

In the dreams and visions of the human mind also continues the evolution of life. It is a matter of being in tune with what is there, to move past the surface into the depth of living systems. It is a profoundly religious experience. The connotation of the word "religion" is to respect what is sacred, and what is sacred for American Indians is nature. Bron Taylor, who was well aware of American Indian and other Indigenous ways of seeing and relating with nature, used the phrase "Dark Green Religion" to refer to the spiritual orientation of Deep Ecology.[280] It is, he argues, central to the environmental moment. It is reflected in the writings of Thoreau, John Muir, Aldo Leopold, Gary Snyder, and many other leading figures of the environmental movement, and it informs the motivational passion of groups like Earth First! and Greenpeace, among others.

But long before these developments in Anglo-American society, it stood as an integral part of Indigenous culture and is central to American Indian religious philosophy, which is one of the roots of the contemporary emerging concept, while the direct experience of those involved in the environmental movement is another.

Embedded in religion is morality, and so it is that within Deep Green Religion is deep green morality. This eco-centered morality is innate to organic relations. By contrast Western philosophical ethics is synthetic, an artifact of city life, and anthropocentric. The various theories of ethics in Western intellectual history are confined to human relations, whereas the nonhuman world has no ethical standing apart for human concerns. Thus it is that from Aristotle through Kant, animals have no value in themselves, but only utilitarian value for human use. Aristotle asserts that wild animals have less value than domesticated animals because they are of less benefit to man. For Kant the only ground for ethical concern for animals is how they relate to rational man. Animals in the wild and wild nature are amoral at best. For those who have concern for ecology and animal welfare, there is little support in Western historical thought on which to draw.

Environmental Ethics

With the advent of the environmental crisis, there is in turn a need for an environmental ethics. To this end one of the earliest responses among Anglo-Americans is the concept of "Land Ethic." The basic idea was introduced into the environmental movement by Aldo Leopold with his 1949 publication of *A Sand County Almanac*. In it he expresses the need to expand ethical concern beyond just humanity to include ecology. He writes, "The land ethic simply enlarges the boundaries of community to include soils, water, plants, and animals, or collectively: the land."[281] Aware that the history of civilization has been one of conquest and domination over nature, he goes on to write that "a land ethic changes the role of Homo sapiens from conqueror of the land-community to plain member."[282]

He uses the word "citizen" as a metaphor for this membership, which is problematic given its root meaning, but then again it is a metaphor directed to civilized people who need to change in order to be healthy members of a biotic community. It is civilization that needs to change to adapt to nature. The project of changing nature to meet the supposed needs of civilization is the root cause of the problem. Leopold points out that conservation alone is insufficient if it is driven by human economic concern without regard for nature as being of intrinsic value. "One basic weakness in a conservation system based wholly on economic motives is that most members of the land community have no economic value."[283] This is to say that an anthropocentric ethic cannot sufficiently serve the common good of all members of a biotic community. What is needed is an eco-centric ethics of the kind that American Indians have, which is deeply rooted in the land.

Baird Callicott, a major contributor to the environmental movement and the development of environmental ethics, is both a scholar of Leopold's land ethic and of American Indian environmental philosophy. He argues that the two are complementary, and identifies three areas of significant overlap:

> First, the primary feature of the land ethic is the representation of nature as congeries of societies and of human-nonhuman relationships as essentially social [Mitakuye Oyas'in].... Second, it is social membership to which ethics and ethical attitudes are correlative.

For American Indians this means being in relationship with all our ancestors, both human and nonhuman, so that there is ethical responsibility for all living beings throughout nature. For Leopold it means that the individual is a member of a community of inter-dependent parts. The third point has the greatest implications for academic philosophers, that "Leopold takes a more Humean than Kantian approach to the concept of ethics and morality."[284]

Callicott seems to imply here that an American Indian ethic is agreeable to a Humean understanding. On the surface this seems questionable, as David Hume was a Western philosopher much dif-ferent in cultural genera from Indigenous philosophizing, but as contrasted with Kant, there is far more similarity with Hume. It is certainly the case that Leopold's ethic has its epistemic grounding in a Humean understanding.

David Hume was personally acquainted with Rousseau and like him broke with the dominant paradigm of Western thought. It may be that Hume, like Rousseau, was influenced by the extensive dis-cussion of American Indians in Europe at that time.[285] The Western tradition from ancient Greece to modernity held reason to be the measure of what is good. From Pythagoras, and reiterated in Plato, we get a moral dualism of good versus evil, so that the organic is the locus of evil and the good is located in a transcendental domain of pure rational thought.

This view has older roots in Zoroastrianism, which came to influence Judaism around the time of Christ and became inte-grated into Christian theology. The additional synthesis of Greek philosophy with Christian theology equated the logos with God and the natural world with Satan. The Hebrew meaning of the word "satan" means to oppose. With reason associated with God, then, that which is opposed to such is the irrational; thus nature is believed to be evil.

Modern philosophy is more agnostic about matters of theology but continues to associate morality with rationality and the immoral with the irrational; moreover, modern philosophy holds that human beings are born without reason and must be subdued and improved into reason, in opposition to their inborn natural incli-nations. Hume calls all this into question, asserting that reason in and of itself cannot be the source of morality. He held that rational thought can be good at establishing facts, and, so, is indispensable to science, but there is nothing inherent in facts that entail morals.

Morality resides in sentiments such as empathy, compassion, love, and the like. In other words, one cannot derive an "ought" from an "is"—since ought is not definable by logic apart from feelings. In this view, one can establish the facts of manmade global warming and climate change or the increasing presence of toxic health treating chemicals in the environment from industrial sources, but this in and of itself says nothing about what ought to be done.[286]

In a Humean perspective, the science of ecology can provide facts but not values; for a moral response one needs Deep Ecology based on feeling values. Leopold writes:

> It is inconceivable to me that an ethical relation to land can exist without love, respect, and admiration for land and a high regard for its [moral] value.[287]

It is the love of the natural world that is axiomatic to the moral sentiment of American Indian ecology and for Euro-American environmentalists like Thoreau, Leopold, Muir, and many others. Focusing on love of nature as foundational to a moral understanding requires a more holistic approach to distinguishing right from wrong. Leopold offers such a standard:

> A thing is right when it tends to preserve the integrity, stability, and beauty of the biotic community. It is wrong when it tends otherwise.[288]

This statement is descriptive of an Indigenous ethics. Goodness in aboriginal society is communal in nature and based on harmonious relationships. The phrase "the good of the people" is used in Indian country with much frequency. In the aboriginal sense "the people" are inclusive of both humans and nonhumans, since all relationships are within an ecological whole.

As has been becoming increasingly clear to a growing number of people, the relationship of human beings to their environment is critical, and contemporary society has fallen into a dangerous disharmony with the environment. Or more accurately, human activity has been causing the environment to be disharmonious for many species, including human beings.

The current situation is unsustainable! While many are in denial, some seek out alternatives. To this end American Indian ecological philosophy seems possibly to offer something of an answer, and thus has been, directly and indirectly, a major source of inspiration for the current environmental movement. Most Americans, however, know little about the actual situation of American Indians, as their nations and members engage in an effort at renewal, after the horrendous physical and cultural geno- cide they experienced.[289]

Early Indian Participation in the Environmental Movement

Past influences of American Indians have been an important source of worldview and ideas for many Americans engaged in the environmental movement, along with writings by Indians, includ- ing some mentioned earlier in this chapter, and an increasing num- ber of books, films, and other media about them (discussed in the introduction to part II of this book, below). In some cases contact with Indians has had a direct influence in moving people toward an Indigenous environmental consciousness.

An interesting example of this is Archibald Belaney.[290] He was born in England in 1888, and moved to Canada early in the twen- tieth century. For some time he functioned as a trapper, having learned some of the skills involved, as well as harvesting techniques, in his studies of the Ojibwe. Then, he developed a relationship with a young Haudenosaunee woman, Gertrude Bernard, who played a major role in his transition from trapper to conservationist. As Belaney became Indianized, identifying with First Nations people, he took the name Grey Owl (or Wa-sha-quon-asin, from the Ojibwe wenjiganooshiinh, meaning "great horned owl" or "great grey owl").

As Grey Owl, Belaney gained prominence as a conservationist well beyond Canada, lecturing, writing numerous articles and books, and making and being depicted in numerous films. In 1931, at Riding National Park in Manitoba, he became caretaker of park animals. He had a major impact as what today would be considered a deep green conservationist, challenging people to reevaluate their relationship with the natural world. He pointed out the destructive impact of human beings on nature in their commodification of nature's fruits for profit, and the need to develop a deep respect for the natural world.

In addition, numerous Indians have long been engaged in efforts to protect the environment, reminding us that we are part of it, intimately connected to all beings, contributing directly to the environmental movement.

Of particular note is that the Hopi prophecies had for eons spoken of a great weapon, a gourd of ashes—clearly an environmental threat—that would burn the Earth and boil the ocean, as well as other cataclysmic environmental threats. To avoid these cataclysms, the Hopi needed to go to the "house of mica" on the eastern shore of Turtle Island (North America), where representatives of the peoples of the Earth would meet to discuss what to do about the threat of the great weapon, and other dangers.[291]

It was said that the Hopi needed to go and attempt to share their prophecies up to four times at that place, but if they were not heard by the fourth visit, the result would be tremendous destruction. It was not clear until August 6, 1945, that it became apparent that the gourd of ashes was an atomic bomb, and shortly after that, that the house of mica was the United Nations. Beginning in 1948, four Hopi ambassadors, one of whom was Thomas Banyacya, were appointed by one of the Hopi Kivas (ceremonial societies) to take the prophecies to the outside world, which they did regularly, speaking at numerous conferences and events for many years. Banyacya and others formed a Hopi delegation that began going to the UN. On those four visits they were given only a polite listening. However, UNESCO supported the translation and printing in several languages of a publication of a book about the prophecies, Thomas E. Mails and Dan Evehema, *Hotevilla: Hopi Shrine of the Covenant, Microcosm of the World*, published in 1995.

Since then the UN has become extremely involved in environmental issues, particularly climate change, as is discussed below. Often, Banyacya teamed with members of other Indian nations in speaking at various public meetings and conferences about a range of issues, including the environment, from a Native perspective.[292]

Thus, well before the environmental movement was effectively launched in the United States, American Indians were active in moving the North American and world publics toward caring about environmental, as well as other, issues. This activity, including strong direct focus on environmental concerns, has continued to expand, soon including Indians from throughout the Americas and Indigenous people from around the world.[293]

One of the early major international Indian efforts took place in 1977, when a delegation of American Indians traveled to Geneva, Switzerland, to testify before a United Nation conference on "Discrimination against the Indigenous Population of the Americas." For this conference John Mohawk, a Seneca elder in collaboration with other elders of the Haudenosaunee, wrote a message to the Western world entitled *A Basic Call to Consciousness*, published by *Akwesasne Notes*:

In the beginning we were told that human beings who walk about on the Earth have been provided with all the things necessary for life. We were instructed to carry a love for one another and to show a great respect for all the beings of the earth ... [with the original instructions directing] that we who walk about on the Earth are to express a great respect, affection, and gratitude toward all the spirits which create and support Life. We give a greeting and thanksgiving to the many supporters of our lives—the corn, beans, squash, the wind, the sun.[294]

The message goes on to note that not all people have the same respect: "The Indo-European people who have colonized our lands have shown very little respect for the things that create and support Life."[295] The original homeland of the Indo-European is in the steppes of Russia. These are a people who invented a militarized sociopolitical system called "patriarchy."

This contention is supported by the archaeological work of Professor Marija Gimbutas, who gives a detailed mapping of the spread of Indo-European patriarchy across western Eurasia.[296] She points to evidence that prior to the arrival of patriarchal society, people followed an Earth Goddess religion and lived at peace with nature. These earlier cultures lived in villages along waterways with little to no fortification or evidence of much in the way of weaponry. This changed with the spread of patriarchy. With patriarchy a pattern of warfare militarized these cultures. In the process the old religion gave way to the newer male-centered warrior religions glorifying violence and conquest.

The primary mode of economy for these ancient Indo-Europeans was domestication of animals. "Herding and breeding of animals signaled a basic alteration in the relationship of human to other life forms."[297] As noted above, the attitude of domination and control evolved from domestication. That attitude would come to infect the Semitic tribes to the south, an agricultural people who developed a system of irrigation in order to increase production to meet expanding population as the villages were growing into cities. With this we see the beginning of the earliest civilizations. The political system was moving toward becoming a hierarchical military structure of command and control, with class division and a warrior king as supreme ruler. The mythology would come to reflect this sociopolitical culture. God, who began as a war totem, became the supreme ruler of the universe, thus marking the birth of monotheism.

The Haudenosaunee's message goes on to report the destructive effects of all this as it led to genocide and ecocide. Western civilization "has been horribly exploitative and destructive on the Natural World." It has led to the mass extinction of hundreds, perhaps thousands, of species and caused many more, such as the buffalo, to be drastically reduced in number. Water and air have been polluted, becoming a major health issue. The forests were leveled: less than a tenth of the original forests are still standing, and this is under siege.

> Western technology and the people who have employed it have been the most amazingly destructive force in all of human history.... Western Civilization is on a death path on which their own culture has no viable answers. When faced with the reality of their own destructiveness, they can only go forward into areas of more efficient destruction.[298]

In Jerry Mander's book *In the Absence of the Sacred: The Failure of Technology and the Survival of the Indian Nations,* there is the thesis that modern technology is inseparable from the historical ideology that produced it. There is the Baconian project to torture Mother Nature to yield her secrets, in order to create technology to have control over her.

Then there is the agenda of subdue and improve, of domination and control. Perhaps most important as a precursor to industrialization is the mechanical worldview, which on the one hand serves as a model for the machinery of industry, and on the other reduces nature to a mute, lifeless resource to do with as one wills. In other words, with such a view, nature cannot be sacred. It is just a thing, so we have no direct ethical concern for it, but are free to use it for human-devised ends. This is the underlying philosophy of modernity, and this is what both Jerry Mander and John Mohawk are critical of in pointing out the extreme destructive effects. From *A Basic Call to Consciousness*:

The air is foul, the waters poisoned, the trees dying, the animals are disappearing. We think even the systems of weather are changing. Our ancient teaching warned us that if Man interfered with the Natural laws, these things would come to be.[299]

Differing Approaches to Natural Law

The concept of "natural law" is used here to refer to behavioral norms conforming to the original instructions. At the UN conference in Geneva, in addition to the Haudenosaunee representatives, the participants included Hopis, Lakota, Guaimi, Cheyenne, Ojibwe, Aymara, Muskogee, Quichua, Apache, Cree, and many more. They stood together in solidarity, agreeing that there are natural laws which provide a normative standard for proper behavior. As Native commentators have pointed out, there is also a Western tradition of the concept dating back to Stoicism in ancient Greece and Rome.

Thomas Aquinas built upon it to develop a Christian version of natural law ethics.[300] His position is that the universe is so designed by God's will as to entail a moral norm, thus morality is not an arbitrary invention of manmade society, but is transhistorical and transcultural, emanating from God. Morality is universal; therefore, right and wrong are not relative but apply to all equally.

Consider for example the concept of "crimes against humanity" used in reference to the Holocaust and other such events. The Universal Declaration of Human Rights, established as international law by the United Nations, is based on natural law ethics. It does, however, remain anthropocentric: only humans have rights and there is no declaration of ecological rights apart from human concern. As Indigenous commentators have urged the West to rediscover for itself, Indigenous natural law ethics are eco-centered, and the integrity of ecology has moral standing. Another difference is that the ethics of Aquinas, and those akin to him, are founded on reason as given by a supernatural deity, and so it is not altogether natural. An Indigenous natural law is based on intuitive feelings emanating from pantheistic animism. This is a more Humean-like moral sentiment being found in biological nature.

The Medicine Wheel

The ethical norms of Native America are woven into the Sacred Hoop as the Medicine Wheel. This Medicine Wheel may serve as a moral compass with its four directions: East, South, West, and North. Each direction symbolizes a complex of meaning. While there are tribal, clan, family, and individual variations, for many, the directions are often seen in this way. The East symbolizes the rising sun, thus beginnings, of springtime and birth and the growing awareness of the surrounding world. The South is associated with midday, with summer and warmth, with childhood and feelings. The West belongs to sunset, autumn, the coming of age, and intuitive introspection. The North is the place of midnight, old age, and the wisdom of elders and ancestors. At the center of the Wheel is the axis which connects Mother Earth and Father Sky.

According to the teachings of Great Harmony, each direction ought to be in balance with the others, and they relate in pairs such as East and West. The way of the East on the Wheel must be balanced with its complementary opposite in the West, which is to say that awareness of the world outside must be balanced with the introspective space within. Likewise, the wisdom of the North needs to be balanced with the playful feelings of the warm summer's childlike spontaneity. Most important, the masculinity of Father Sky must be balanced with the femininity of Mother Earth.

In contrast, the pathology of civilization is with patriarchy, whereby the masculine energy is given all, and femininity is oppressed and repressed with a militant misogyny. Also hyperrationality creates an imbalance with the feelings of the South, and European thought has been icy cold like a winter wind. Conditions like these create disharmony between oneself and the world. It is what produces the alienation that civil humanity feels toward nature.

The balance and harmony of the Medicine Wheel reflect balance and harmony with nature. The modern environmental crisis is a world out of balance. This is central to understanding the Hopi prophecy. The Hopi, like most other Indian tribes, have a set of teachings that includes, in a specific way, the wisdom of the Medicine Wheel. The Hopi prophecy is a mytho-poetic expression of what in Indigenous thinking are the original instructions, along with diagnostic description of what happens when the world diverges from that norm, thus becoming out of balance. It is particularly pointed in warnings about the harmful effects of excessive technological manipulation of the natural world. A number of books and films, as well as elders and others speaking publicly, have contributed to the environmental movement, in making aspects of the Hopi prophecies more widely known.[301]

The Hopi formed a spiritual and political alliance with the Haudenosaunee to bring the message to the United Nations that the world is out of balance and heading on a destructive course. Hopi elder David Monongwe, representing his people, became friends with John Mohawk, finding much in common on core ecological values. The Hopi prophecies suggest that if the catastrophe is to be lessened, for its beginnings are already upon us, then the Anglo-Americans must become Indigenous, that is to say, live in harmony with the natural world.

More Recent American Indian Contributions to the Environmental Movement

A great many other American Indians have also been working to restore balanced relations between human beings and the Earth. Some have been doing this in their own communities and neighboring areas. For example, Eastern Navajo Diné Against Uranium Mining (ENDAUM) has long worked to protect water on the Navajo Reservation from uranium mining and related activities. In 2004, numerous members testified at a hearing of the New Mexico State Water Quality Control Commission (NMWQCC), in favor of lowering the amount of permitted uranium in water under the state's groundwater-protection standard for uranium by nearly two hundred times. This helped the commission reach that decision in early June, that year.[302]

Similarly, in an effort to protect endangered salmon, sacred to their tribes and an important food and income source, members of the Karuk, Yurok, Hoopa, and Klamath Tribes and staffers from Friends of the River and the Pacific Coast Federation of Fishermen's Associations undertook an email campaign on July 21, 2004, to Scottish Power Board of Directors, shortly before their annual shareholders meeting. The campaign informed them that their American subsidiary, PacifiCorp, owner of dams on the Klamath River, was not living up to the company's "green" standards.[303] The dams on the Klamath River owned and operated by PacifiCorp blocked access to more than 350 miles of historic spawning habitat. The Klamath dams were in the process of being relicensed by the federal government.

On July 27, 2004, Native Americans demonstrated in Edinburgh, calling for the placement of fish ladders or other measures on Klamath River dams to allow salmon to move upstream. In addition, the Yurok Tribe organized a demonstration for the FERC hearings on Klamath River dams in Eureka, California, on June 22, 2004, during public commentary before federal regulatory agencies on an application by PacifiCorp/Scottish Power to continue operating Klamath River dams for power generation. The tribe, fishermen, and conservationists sought removal of the low-power output dams because of their severe direct and indirect impacts on salmon, other fisheries, and the health of the entire river ecosystem. These actions were major contributions to decisions to remove these dams.

Among the many individual Indigenous North Americans involved in environmental activism, Winona LaDuke, member of the Red Lake Band of Chippewa Indians in Minnesota, worked to redevelop wild rice growing on the reservation. She also founded the White Earth Reclamation Project for the tribe to regain and steward land lost during the allotment process, and to overcome environmental racism.[304] She joined with Indigo Girls Amy Ray and Emily Saliers in 1993 to found Honor the Earth, to address the two primary needs of the Native environmental movement: the need to break the geographic and political isolation of Native communities and the need to increase financial resources for organizing and change. Honor the Earth's website states:

> As a unique national Native initiative, Honor the Earth works to a) raise public awareness and b) raise and direct funds to grassroots Native environmental groups. We are the only Native organization that provides both financial support and organizing support to Native environmental initiatives. This model is based on strategic analysis of what is needed to forge change in Indian country, and it is based deep in our communities, histories, and long-term struggles to protect the earth.[305]

LaDuke, who also has served on the board of directors of Greenpeace, and with Honor the Earth, has been involved with environmental issues, particularly concerning Native people, throughout the United States and beyond, and has spoken and published widely on these concerns. This has included Honor the Earth, in coordination with Solar Energy International, the Western Shoshone Defense Project, American Spirit Productions, and the Battle Mountain Band of Te-Moak Western Shoshone providing free training and installation of a solar photovoltaic system in Western Shoshone territory near Elko, Nevada, in April 2005.[306]

Renowned Salish and Kootenai Nation artist Jaune Quick-to-See Smith often uses her art to address current issues in tribal politics, human rights, and environmental issues with humor. She dedicated her Chief Seattle series of mixed media collages in the late 1980s and early 1990s to educating viewers on environmental issues.[307] Smith has received numerous awards for her work, and put on more than one hundred solo exhibits. It has been said of her, "Smith is skilled at creating and appropriating texts that capture the paradigms of American society in ways that reveal the cultural implications of capitalism, historic amnesia, and assignment of racial categories."[308] That has certainly been the case with artful illustration in the Chief Seattle series, for mainstream society to become aware of what it has been doing to the environment and to take corrective action.

Numerous tribes, in addition to acting against pollution on, and entering, their reservations, have moved to install renewable energy programs. A few of the many examples include: The Morongo Band of Mission Indians is constructing a wind generation station to meet their own and surrounding community power needs. The Navajo Nation is including wind power in its energy development program, though there has been controversy over its plan to also build a new coal-fired electric generation plant, even though it will be much less polluting of the air (but not in terms of carbon dioxide) than older coal-fueled facilities. Laguna Pueblo designer Dave Melton and Sacred Power Corporation of Albuquerque, of which he is co-owner, are bringing electricity to isolated homes on the Navajo Reservation in New Mexico, using wind turbines and photovoltaic cells. And, the Hopi Nation is installing both wind and photovoltaic electric power generation.[309] Some Indian nations have also been working to capture methane— a potent greenhouse gas, if allowed to escape into the air—from landfills—to use as fuel.[310]

Tribal members working in government, especially in the US Environmental Protection Administration (EPA), have contributed significantly to protecting the environment. This includes taking leadership in getting the EPA to act on a provision put into the law largely as a result of Indian organization lobbying that federally recognized tribes, which are entities in US federalism, be treated as states for certain purposes. Thus, the EPA began authorizing prepared tribes to do water and air quality regulation, including regulating off-reservation sources of pollution that flows onto reservations.[311]

Tribal members in education, especially in tribal colleges, and the colleges and their programs, have also been important contributors in preserving and restoring the environment. A number of them in the United States have been engaged in research into how their nations can respond to climate change, in some cases in partnership with the US Geological Survey. They created the organization Native View while including study of the changing environment in their curricula. They have been integrating traditional and Western scientific knowledge, doing what they can with limited budgets to make their campuses green, from recycling to improving energy efficiency and reducing pollution.[312] Among them, in one of many such instances, Northwest Indian College offers a bachelor of science in Native environmental science.[313]

Because environmental issues have been so important to Indian tribes, all of the broadly focused US Indian organizations, such the National Congress of American Indians (NCAI),[314] have included environmental protection in their programs. NCAI, for example, has called for stronger US environmental measures, and increased authority for tribes to undertake environmental regulation, in its proposals to the US Congress.

Numerous other Indian organizations have had a more direct focus on protecting and renewing the environment. The Intertribal Council on Utility Policy, for instance, an organization composed of federally recognized Indian tribes in the northern Great Plains, has been among those organizations supporting the growth of wind-powered electric generation. They have contributed to wind power development among a number of Great Plains Tribes for years.[315] Others include the National Tribal Environmental Council (NTEC); the Institute for Tribal Environmental Professionals (ITEP), which works to strengthen tribal capacity and sovereignty in environmental and natural resource management through culturally relevant education, research, partnerships, and policy-based services; the National Environmental Coalition of Native

Americans (NECONA), Native American environmentalists working to keep nuclear waste off Indian lands; Native American Fish
and Wildlife Society; Native American Water Association; Northwest
Indian Fisheries Commission (NWIFC); and the Indigenous
Environmental Network (IEN).[316]

Expanding International Indigenous Environmental Activism

IEN was established in 1990 within the United States by grassroots
Indigenous peoples and individuals to address environmental and
economic justice issues. However, its focus has become more international, matching the growth of the environmental crisis. This
has included IEN's joining Indigenous organizations from around
the world at the Paris COP21 world climate negotiations, participating in an "Indigenous Press Conference Demanding True Climate
Solutions at COP21," and joining in demonstrations supporting
that demand, in which Indigenous people played a leading role.[317]

Globalization has expanded certain aspects of the environmental crisis, most especially global warming–induced climate
change, and spread various kinds of environmental degradation.
Multinational corporations, for example, have been involved in
building inefficient fossil fuel–burning power stations and factories
in developing nations, while contributing in those nations to deforestation and other serious environmental damage in the course of
mining, oil and gas extraction, and dam construction.[318] Generally,
these destructive activities have been most greatly impacting
Indigenous peoples and other poor communities around the world.

Increasingly there has been an international Indigenous
response, including by numerous organizations from across the
Americas. One channel for this, among a number of international
venues, has been the United Nations, in which, for many years,
Indigenous peoples have joined others in raising and discussing
environmental issues. This includes the UN NGO/DPI Conference,
"Climate Change: How It Impacts Us All," which included two

Indigenous sessions. As a follow-up the conference, the UN secretary general established a Climate Change Caucus of working groups, including an Indigenous Working Group, to make recommendations for action on climate change.[319]

A more important vehicle has been the United Nations Permanent Forum on Indigenous Issues (UNPFII), which has met every spring at UN Headquarters in New York City since 2002.[320] The forum has included considerable discussion of environmental issues at every session. There have also been two UN Indigenous decades, highlighting Indigenous—including environmental—issues; the establishment of the International Declaration of the Rights of Indigenous Peoples; and UN climate change efforts in which Indigenous people and organizations have participated to varying degrees, sometimes setting up intercessional Indigenous working groups. In all of this, Indigenous peoples, including from the Americas, have been able to contribute to the environmental movement.[321]

Pope Francis's Encyclical on Climate Change: A Seminal Event

Perhaps the most seminal set of events concerning American Indians' impact (along with other Indigenous peoples' impact) on the environmental movement has been Pope Francis's Environmental Encyclical, and subsequent apologies to Indigenous peoples and statements about their role in preserving the environment. Jorge Mario Bergoglio, who, at seventy-six, became the first pope from the Americas, lived in Argentina. He was a Jesuit, and archbishop of Buenos Aires. He traveled extensively on the subway and by bus during the fifteen years of his episcopal ministry, which, like his papacy, has a focus on the poor.[322] Thus, he had the opportunity to know Indigenous people well. He was well aware of the problems they faced: being forced from their lands for development; often suffering from uncontrolled pollution from mining or oil drilling;

too often having their lands stripped bare by deforestation, or flooded by dams, which harmed the fish many needed to live.

Having taken the name Francis, stemming from Saint Francis, for his papacy, it is not surprising that he focused on the poor, including Indigenous people. He saw global warming–induced climate change and other environmental degradation mistreating the Earth as being interlinked with mistreatment of the poor, stemming from an anthropocentric lifestyle that was pushing life out of balance. Thus, on the cusp of the Summer Solstice, June 18, 2015, Pope Francis delivered his Environmental Encyclical, "Laudato Si' of the Holy Father Francis on the Care for Our Common Home," which reads as an Indigenous statement:[323]

> Our Sister, Mother Earth, who sustains and governs us, and who produces various fruit with colored flowers and herbs ... now cries out to us because of the harm we have inflicted on her by our irresponsible use and abuse of the goods with which God has endowed her .... We must again speak the "language of fraternity and beauty in our relationship with the world."

Thus the pope called for all people to meet "the urgent challenge to protect our common home," which "includes a concern to bring the whole human family together to seek a sustainable and integral development," protecting the Earth and lifting up the poor (including Indigenous peoples), who suffer most from the shortsighted degradation of the environment, the home of us all. Converging a number of pressing environmental, economic, social, and political concerns, the Encyclical calls for a renewed sense of unity between religion and science, in moving from destructive consumerism to a more balanced way of living.

Pope Francis included important comments about the rights of Indigenous people in the course of discussing the need for modern societies to return to a more balanced way of living:

On care for our common home. It is essential to show special care for indigenous communities and their cultural traditions. They are not merely one minority among others, but should be the principal dialogue partners, especially when large projects affecting their land are proposed.

For them, land is not a commodity but rather a gift from God and from their ancestors who rest there, a sacred space with which they need to interact if they are to maintain their identity and values.

When they remain on their land, they themselves care for it best. Nevertheless, in various parts of the world, pressure is being put on them to abandon their homelands to make room for agricultural or mining projects which are undertaken without regard for the degradation of nature and culture.

The Holy Father Francis made his message even clearer when he spoke to many thousands of people in an open-air mass in the city of San Cristóbal, in Chiapas, in southern Mexico, where three-quarters of the population is Indigenous, on February 15, 2016.[324] The mass was delivered in three native languages (Tzeltal, Tzotzil, and Ch'ol), after a new Vatican decree approved their use.

The pope denounced the greed that has driven the exploitation of the country's Indigenous population and the land that they inhabit:

On many occasions, in a systematic and organized way, your people have been misunderstood and excluded from society.

Some have considered your values, cultures, and traditions inferior. Others, dizzy with power, money, and the laws of the market, have stripped you of your lands and then contaminated them. How sad this is. How worthwhile it would be for each of us to examine our conscience and learn to say, "Forgive me!"

After pausing, the pope added: "Sorry brothers."

Pope Francis also specifically called on the Indigenous people of Chiapas to "teach mankind how to maintain a harmonious relationship with nature," as they have done for generations, with the planet facing "one of the greatest environmental crises in history"—reiterating one of his favored themes.

> The environmental challenge that we are experiencing and its human causes affects us all and demands our response. We can no longer pretend to be deaf in the face of one of the greatest environmental crises in history.
>
> In this you have much to teach, to teach mankind. You know how to maintain a harmonious relationship with nature, and respect it as a source of food, a common home, and an altar for how to share resources among people.

Pope Francis offered a similar apology in 2015 to the Native peoples of the Americas:

> Not only for the offenses of the church herself, but also for crimes committed against the native peoples during the so-called conquest of America. There was sin and an abundant amount of it.

Standing Rock: Increased American Indian Leadership in the Environmental Movement

A major increase in American Indian leadership in the environmental movement in the United States and worldwide took place with the 2016 Indian lead protests against the Dakota Access Pipeline in the vicinity of the Standing Rock Sioux Reservation in North Dakota, with supporting demonstrations around the United States and in many other countries.[325] The prelude to Standing Rock was the rise of concern among Indian nations and environmentalists in the western United States and Canada regarding the water pollution that occurs from the breaks and leaks that occur, fairly frequently, in pipelines carrying oil.

In addition, global warming had become a major concern, especially after the 2015 Paris Climate Change Conference and agreement. Among environmentalists, including Indians and many in larger publics, there was a concern that building new pipelines would lead to increased burning of oil, producing more atmosphere-heating carbon dioxide. Thus, several Canadian tribes had refused to have oil pipelines cross their reserves, while there had been protests against new oil pipelines being built in the United States.[326]

The Dakota Access Pipeline (DAPL) was announced to the public in 2014. It was to be built by Dakota Access LLC, a subsidiary of Energy Transfer Partners from the Bakken shale oil fields in North Dakota, across South Dakota and Iowa to the oil tank farm near Patoka, Illinois. The Meskwaki Tribe in Iowa and several Lakota tribes in the Dakotas strongly opposed the pipeline for environmental reasons, and because the construction and possible oil leaks would threaten sacred sites along the pipeline's route.

A major protest against the construction of DAPL developed in North Dakota in spring 2016. The Standing Rock Sioux Tribe led protests against the construction on land just outside the reservation on several grounds. The first were environmental: the threat to the drinking water of the tribe and a great many people downstream from a spill where or near where the pipe would run under Lake Oahe on the Missouri River. There was also concern that less extreme, but still important damage that would occur from spills elsewhere. Additionally important was the increase in global warming that would result from the large amount of oil that the pipeline would add to that available on the world market. The second set of objections involved tribal sovereignty and culture: that the land at the site of the protest where the construction was taking place was sacred land that would be disturbed by the construction; that the land in question, though outside the reservation and treated by the US government as private land, by treaty belonged to the tribe, which had never given up its ownership. Regardless of that, the tribe had not been properly and sufficiently consulted about the pipeline by the agencies that had approved it.

By fall 2016 the peaceful protest had received a great deal of attention in the United States and worldwide. At its height several thousand people were participating. This included a great many members of at least three hundred Indian nations in the United States and Canada. Among them were more than one thousand US military veterans who came to nonviolently protect the protesters. As a result, more than five hundred tribes in the United States and Canada formally supported the Standing Rock Sioux Tribe's opposition to DAPL, and opposed the construction of new pipelines across Indian lands.

There were several protest camps. Some were off reservation near the construction site, though the Sacred Stone Camp was organized by the Standing Rock Sioux Tribe on their reservation near the area. The camp was run by the tribe, with collaboration from elders of other Indian nations as a cooperative community, stressing peaceful protest, using only nonviolent means while undertaking prayer. The other camps functioned in a similar manner. Anyone who acted violently, or otherwise behaved seriously inappropriately, was banished from the camps.

On September 3, 2016, Dakota Access LLC brought in a private security firm as the company put its bulldozers to work digging up part of the pipeline route that the Standing Rock Sioux claimed held tribal grave sites, while a motion filed by the tribe's attorneys to enjoin construction on that site was pending in court. When unarmed protesters entered the site, security guards attacked them with pepper spray and dogs. At least six peaceful protesters were treated for dog bites. Police observing the security guards attack took no action. The incident was filmed by Amy Goodman and a crew from *Democracy Now* who aired the footage, reporting the event on television and radio.[327] Security experts and civil liberties experts stated that the security firm's actions were completely inappropriate.

In May 2017, public documents and leaked internal memos revealed that TigerSwan, hired by Dakota Access LLC to provide security, had colluded with local, state, and federal law enforcement as they performed "military-style counterterrorism measures" to suppress the protesters, compiled information to assist prosecutors in building cases against protesters, while employing social media in an attempt to sway public support for the pipeline. The media campaign attempted to label the protesters, comparing them with jihadis, and insinuating that those opposing the pipeline were "an ideologically driven insurgency with a strong religious component."[328] TigerSwan continued their social media campaign after the protests had ended at Standing Rock, stressing that there was a growing opposition to pipelines across the United States.

Beginning in August, numerous peaceful protesters were arrested, along with a number of members of the news media, including Amy Goodman, who were merely reporting on the event, and the equipment of some journalists was confiscated. By mid-October more than 140 protesters had been arrested, and there were numerous complaints of harsh and improper treatment by the police of those detained.

On October 27, local police from several agencies, state troopers, and North Dakota National Guard troops, assisted by law officers from neighboring states, with armored personnel carriers, mace, concussion grenades, Tasers, and batons, began an operation to clear out a protest camp and remove blockades from a highway. Amnesty International published a press release on October 28, stating in part:

> These people should not be treated like the enemy. Police must keep the peace using minimal force appropriate to the situation. Confronting men, women, and children while outfitted in gear more suited for the battlefield is a disproportionate response. Under International law and standards, arrests should not be used to intimidate or prevent people from participating in peaceful assembly.[329]

Numerous civil liberty and environmental organizations complained of the actions of Dakota Access LLC and law enforcement. The protests became widely reported and were supported by demonstrations in hundreds of cities, often involving hundreds of participants. Among numerous days of peaceful civic action were the November 15 "National Day of Action,"[330] and on Thanksgiving Day people went from many places around the United States to Standing Rock in support of the protest.[331] On several occasions protests were held at the various headquarters of the US Army Engineers, at which time petitions were delivered asking the engineers not to approve a permit for the Dakota Access Pipeline to be built under Lake Oahe.[332]

On November 14, the Army Engineers released the following statement:

> The Army has determined that additional discussion and analysis are warranted in light of the history of the Great Sioux Nation's dispossessions of lands, the importance of Lake Oahe to the Tribe, our government-to-government relationship, and the statute governing easements through government property.[333]

Then on December 4, the assistant secretary of the army for civil works, Jo-Ellen Darcy, announced:

> [The] Army will not grant easement for Dakota Access Pipeline crossing.... Although we have had continuing discussion and exchanges of new information with the Standing Rock Sioux and Dakota Access, it's clear that there's more work to do.... The best way to complete that work responsibly and expeditiously is to explore alternate routes for the pipeline crossing.[334]

At that point, the Indian-led environmental movement had won a major victory in the course of a campaign that had brought a great deal of increased energy to the environmental movement.

On January 24, 2017, President Trump, shortly after taking office, signed a presidential memorandum reviving the DAPL and other pipeline construction.[335] DAPL construction was then completed, with oil beginning to flow by the beginning of June 2017.[336] That served to reinvigorate the environmental movement. The organization 350.org reported and commented, almost immediately:

> It's been 48 hours since Trump signed his executive actions on the Keystone XL and Dakota Access pipelines, and already more than 50,000 people have pledged to fight these projects to the end.[337]

Among other public reactions, in March 2017 the Standing Rock Sioux tribe led a four-day protest in Washington, DC, culminating in the Native Nations Rise march on March 10. The protesters marched through the capital, pausing to erect a tipi at Trump International Hotel, and rallied in front of the White House.[338]

Meanwhile, the Lakota Sioux Tribe challenged the operation of DAPL in US district court. On June 14, Judge James Boasberg gave the Lakota Sioux a partial victory, writing in a 91-page opinion:

> The Court agrees that [the Corps] did not adequately consider the impacts of an oil spill on fishing rights, hunting rights, or environmental justice, or the degree to which the pipeline's effects are likely to be highly controversial.[339]

However, the court took no immediate action, saying that before deciding on a remedy, the court need to hold additional hearings. Regardless of the eventual outcome in the case, it was clear, as of August 2017, that environmental activism, and American Indian participation and leadership in it, was continuing to increase. At that time, a number of other Indian-led environmental protests were ongoing.[340]

In Mahwah, New Jersey, the Native-led Split Rock Sweetwater Prayer Camp was acting to try to stop construction of the Pilgrim

Pipeline to carry Bakken oil from Albany, New York, to Linden, New Jersey; while in Tacoma, Washington, the Puyallup Tribe and environmentalists were working to try to prevent building of a liquefied natural gas plant. In addition, as 350.org reported on August 16, 2017:

> Indigenous activists from [the Indigenous organization] Idle No More San Francisco (SF) have been working with 350.org to stand up to Big Oil for years.
>
> These brave warriors live near 5 oil refineries in what is known as the "refinery corridor." This corridor includes California's largest refinery, owned by Chevron. A 2012 explosion put this refinery on the map, sending 15,000 people to the hospital with respiratory problems.
>
> In response, Idle No More SF organized 16 "healing walks" over the last four years....[341]
>
> 350.org has proudly partnered with Idle No More SF in organizing and supporting past healing walks. In the months ahead Idle No More SF will be joining with 350.org and other partner organizations to begin work to stop new tar sands fossil fuel infrastructure projects.
>
> Together, we are also organizing to make sure that California Governor Brown's 2018 Climate Summit lives up to its promises to communities in the refinery corridor.

Meanwhile, resistance to DAPL and other pipelines was expanding in other forms. For example, a nationwide campaign to pressure banks stop investing in pipelines was underway.[342]

American Indian environmental activism was continuing to expand as of the fall of 2019 within the North American environmental movement and its leadership. This has particularly been the case with young Indigenous people participating in the youth-led movement to act on climate change. This was most visible in the worldwide Climate Strike, in which more than 4 million people in the United States, and more than 7.5 million around the world, demonstrated for strong rapid government action to counter global warming during the week of September 20–27, 2019.[343] Among the numerous young Native Americans from many nations in environmental leadership, including in Climate Strike, were Yang (Diné), part of the steering committee for Youth United for Climate Crisis Action (YUCCA); Kimberly Pikok Piquk (Inupiaq), student at the University of Alaska–Fairbanks; Bernadette Demientieff (Gwichyaa Gwich'in), executive director of the Gwich'in Steering Committee in Alaska; Autumn Peltier (Anishinaabe), who used the UN platform to speak about the lack of clean water for Indigenous people in Canada; Xiuhtezcatl Tonatiuh Martinez, a member of a group of young people suing the US government over climate change, and Tokata Iron Eyes of the environmentally focused Lakota People's Law Project who spoke during the January 2019 Washington, DC, Women's March.[344]

The Environmental Movement: Restoring Balance and Harmony with the Natural World

The environmental movement is an effort to restore balance and harmony with the natural world. In other words, it is a movement toward indigenization. Gary Snyder, discussed above in the section on the counterculture, is the American poet of Deep Ecology, and writes of the need for "re-inhabitation." Much of his mytho-poetics is drawn from Indigenous wisdom. For Snyder, to be Indigenous is to attune to ecosystem habitation such that:

> inhibitory people sometimes say "this piece of land is sacred"—or "all the land is sacred." This is an attitude that draws on awareness of the mystery of life and death; of taking life to live; of giving life back—not only to your own children, but to the life of the whole land.[345]

Among the Haudenosaunee there is an ethical standard that any course of action by the people must be reflected in the well-being of the next seven generations inhabiting the land. Clearly modern capitalism, which does extensive damage to ecosystems, does not have such an ethical standard.

Raymond Dasmann, one of the pioneers in developing the conservation concepts of "eco-development" and "biological diversity," emphasized the crucial importance of recognizing Indigenous peoples and their cultures in efforts to conserve natural landscapes.[346] He makes a distinction between what he calls "ecosystem-based culture" and "biosphere cultures," the former being Indigenous and the latter being like modern capitalism.

Of these differences Snyder writes that ecosystem-based societies are:

> centered in terms of natural regions and watersheds, as against those [biosphere cultures] who discovered—seven or eight thousand years ago in a few corners of the globe— that it was "profitable" to spill over into drainage, another watershed, another peoples' territory, and steal away its resources, natural or human.[347]

Biosphere cultures are very disruptive of the ecosystem and unsustainable in the long run, just as the Hopi prophecy warned. And as the Hopi suggested and Snyder echoes, the antidote to this madness is indigenization. This requires Deep Green religious ethics, of which Snyder writes:

> The ethics or morality of this is far more subtle than merely being nice to squirrels.... We must find our way to seeing the mineral cycles, the water cycles, air cycles, nutrimental cycles, as sacramental—and we must incorporate that insight into our own personal spiritual quest and integrate it with all the wisdom teaching we have received from the nearer past.[348]

Seeing the cycles of nature as sacred is to understand the way of the circle. The biosphere culture of the modern techno-industrial economy has, as Barry Commoner said, "broken out of the circle … the end result is the environmental crisis, as crisis of survival." From Thoreau to Snyder there has been this effort to heal the circle, which is to say re-indigenize and re-inhabit the land according to Deep Green religious norms. This is the essence of the environmental movement. This is the mending of the Sacred Hoop. "Once more, to survive we must close the circle."[349] In the course of this movement, American Indians and other Indigenous peoples have played a major role. What this means in terms of changing from biosphere to ecosystem ways of seeing is developed in part II, in chapter 7: "Indigenizing the Greening of the World: Applying an Indigenous Approach to Environmental Issues."

Conclusion to Part I: The Influence of American Indians on Western Politics and Society

Stephen M. Sachs

I n considering questions of influence on human thought and action, it is important to remember that human beings have both an individual and a collective aspect. This has been recognized from early Indigenous societies to the present, though the relative importance and place of each has varied. The difference has been particularly clear between the more individualistic versions of reductionist, either/or, Western thinking and more holistic understandings—including those of American Indians and thinkers of the Native-rooted American philosophy of pragmatism.

To differing degrees and in varying ways, people are creative, unique individuals. At the same time they live in societies and wider environments in which individuals are always dialoguing with each other, changing each other in the process to which they add something from themselves in the context of their experience. We each do our own thinking, and have our own direct personal experience. Our personal experience is both direct and indirect, encompassing all kinds of input from others. But we are simultaneously part of cultures and subcultures that, while continually changing, tend to be to be long-lasting. These cultures function as if they have a life of their own, acting as thought fields, in different ways impacting the people who live within them. Many strands of traditions, ideas, and influence come to us and impact us in different ways to different degrees. Once an idea or way of seeing is established, it tends to continue into the future, as one of many interacting strands—some recognized some not—that may vary in strength or volume over time, depending on many factors.

In this kind of situation it is difficult to know precisely, and often one can only estimate vaguely what has influenced a particular person, and in what ways and to what degrees. Sometimes someone is already thinking in the way an idea is presented to them, and the effect may be anything from a slight or stronger conformation, to a major reinforcement, to a considerable enhancement. At other times, to the extent that a person is open to a new idea or way of seeing, because of their nature combined with their previous experience, ideas may greatly impact them, in part depending on the strength and length of duration of the influence.

Also, there may be no completely new idea or way of seeing, while a very wide range of ideas and worldviews are present to at least some degree at any time in any sizable society or set of social groupings. But unless there is something in the context to be open to it as a new, maintaining, reinforcing, or changing energy, one person's ideas, no matter how well communicated, will not have a significant effect. However, if the inconsequential ideas of one moment are carried forward to a different moment, they may eventually have a strong influence.

While there is always uncertainty about the degree of influence, when there is strong evidence of it, we can hypothesize with a high degree of certainty that influence has taken place, either directly or indirectly, at one time or over time. While American Indians' ways and voices are but one strand of many that interact with the individuals in the West, there is massive evidence that indeed Native Americans and their ways have had, and continue to have, a huge effect on Western, and especially US, culture. This has impacted how we act socially, economically, and politically. Of course, a great many other strands of influence have moved a great deal of

Western thought and action, and continue to do so, in ways that are definitely not Indigenous.

It is now clear that from the very beginning, the first three centuries of contact by Europeans with Indians had profound effects on the people who came to live in the Americas, and in Europe, largely from the huge number of reports received from "the New World." Different people from, and in, different European countries were impacted in varying ways and to different degrees. Europeans developed a variety of views about Indians, some of which were quite inaccurate, creating positive and negative stereotypes. Overall, a number of major, as well as some minor, changes of thinking occurred among European Americans, and at least certain Europeans. These impacts had short-run effects on politics and society, while establishing a number of long-term strands of thought or tradition. Some of these have been major, others important minority views that at certain times have expanded to become important elements of later movements.

There is strong evidence that the idea of human freedom as a set of inalienable rights first stated in the West by Locke resulted from contacts with Indians. That there has been as much democracy as has been in the United States is largely a result of European experience with Indigenous Americans, and this has had a worldwide impact. Locke, who had been the leading political theorist for the various groups from right to left in the mainstream of the United States, learned a great deal from reports about and conversations with Native Americans, which greatly impacted his views.

He was not, however, as democratic as Indians, and how he interpreted what he learned from Indigenous peoples resulted in views of economics that provided much in the way of a theoretical basis for capitalism that was not compatible with Indian values. Locke's treatises on civil government were important supports of the English Revolution and Restoration, which, with their Indian roots, continue to be major elements of Western thinking with ongoing, broad worldwide influence.

Rousseau, who was more favorable to Indians than Locke, while learning from as many sources and peoples as possible, incorporated a great deal of what he gained from Indians into his political theory. This has had a huge impact, including that he was the most important thinker for the French Revolution. Its motto, "Liberty, equality, fraternity," was taken directly from him.

Even more so than Locke, Rousseau has been interpreted in a wide variety of ways, contributing to a range of ideas from participatory democracy to totalitarian democracy (government for the people by a leader or elite who in their view understand the people, and the general will, better than the people do themselves, as some fascists have asserted). However, Rousseau's main lasting Indian-influenced impact includes what in the United States in the 1930s became New Deal liberalism. This approach to political economy was revitalized in the US mainstream with the 2016 presidential campaign and the political movement that grew from it.

Similarly, we have shown that much of the socialist and anarchist traditions have important Native roots that remain very much alive today in European and other social democracies, though there is generally little awareness of those roots.

We have demonstrated that in the colonial period and early years of the United States, European American and later American culture was greatly impacted by Indian ways, and that Indian and Indian-related symbols were in common usage at least through the middle of the nineteenth century. Many of the US "founding fathers" were greatly influenced by Indians and their ways, and US institutions were shaped significantly by Indian influences, some directly and some indirectly by way of Locke and perhaps Montesquieu and later Rousseau. While after the mid-nineteenth century, much of the open references to Native Americans dropped out of US culture, important strands of thought remained strong. This included the continuing unfolding of the American philosophy of pragmatism. Often, these views were important minority opinions, with significant practical application such as John Dewey's launching of progressive education. At times, however, these Native strands have blossomed more broadly, as in the women's movement and in the growth of the environmental movement.

This brings us to the two very important reasons why it is relevant to discuss the huge influence Indians have had on Western politics and society, as well as on other aspects of Western and world life. The first reason is that acknowledging how much the West has learned from Indians will contribute to ending the racism that Native Americans still suffer. The acknowledgment will foster mutual respect, while providing one means for helping to overcome the historical trauma that many Indigenous Americans suffer from the physical and cultural genocide of their peoples.[350] Native people have long been told that their traditional cultures were inferior. Many Indigenous people have internalized this view in a sense of inferiority. With the acknowledgement of what Native cultures have contributed to the world, it becomes clear that they were in many ways superior; and that for the Indigenous peoples and the West, with certain more developed technologies, each has had something to learn from each other.

The second reason that the recognition of American Indian contributions to Western politics and society is important is that Indigenous values and ways of seeing have been becoming increasingly relevant to the world of the twenty-first century, as is demonstrated by the women's, LGBT, and environmental movements. This growing relevance of Indigenous thinking is the subject of part II of this volume.

Notes to Volume II

1. Donald A. Grinde and Bruce E. Johansen, *Exemplar of Liberty: Native Americans and the Evolution of Democracy* (Los Angeles: American Indian Studies Center, University of California, 1991), chaps. 11–12.

2. On the disposition and physical and cultural genocide, see Angie Debo, *A History of the Indians of the United States* (Norman: University of Oklahoma Press, 1970), chaps. 2–19; Robert W. Venables, *American Indian History: Five Centuries of Conflict and Coexistence*, vols. 1–2 (Santa

Fe, NM: Clear Light, 2004); Jake Page, *In the Hands of the Great Spirit: The 20,000 Year History of American Indians* (New York: Free Press, 2003), pts. 2–4; Roger L. Nichols, *American Indians in US History* (Norman: University of Oklahoma Press, 2003), chaps. 2–6; and LaDonna Harris, Stephen M. Sachs, and Barbara Morris, *Re-Creating the Circle: The Renewal of American Indian Self-Determination* (Albuquerque: University of New Mexico Press, 2011), chap. 2.

3. For example, see "Charles Alexander Eastman (Ohiye S'a), 1858–1939," in *American Indian Culture: From Counting Coup to Wampum*, ed. Bruce E. Johansen, vol. 2 (Santa Barbara, CA: Greenwood, 2015), 365–69; "Deloria, Ella Cara (Anpetu Wastewin), Standing Rock Sioux, 1889–1971," in *The Encyclopedia of Native American Biography: Six Hundred Life Stories of Important People, from Powhatan to Wilma Mankiller*, ed. Bruce Johansen and Donald A. Grinde Jr. (New York: Henry Holt, 1997), 105–6.

4. Grinde and Johansen, *Exemplar of Liberty*, 247.

5. Robert Hieronimus and Laura Cortner, *The Secret Life of Lady Liberty: Goddess in the New World* (Rochester, VT: Destiny, 2016), 1–4, 26, 33–34, 43, 51, and chap. 3. Hieronimus and Courtner, *The Secret Life of Lady Liberty*, is a good source for the historical discussion that follows. More detail on the US history of the period, including the ups and downs of slavery, and the taking of land from Indians, can be seen in such works as Henry Steele Commager and Samuel Eliot Morison, *The Growth of the American Republic* (New York: Oxford University Press, 1930), and the later version *Oxford History of the United States*, 7th ed. (New York: Oxford University Press, 1980); Charles Austin Beard, *History of the United States* ([Place of publication not identified]: Pantianos Classics, 1921); Angie Debo, *A History of the Indians of the United States* (Norman: University of Oklahoma Press, 1989); Roger L. Nichols, *American Indians in U. S. History* (Norman: University of Oklahoma Press, 2003); Robert W. Venables, *American Indian History: Five Centuries of Conflict and Coexistence*, vols. 1–2 (Santa Fe, NM: Clear Light, 2004); and Jake Page, *In the Hands of the Great Spirit: The 20,000 Year History of the American Indians* (New York: Free Press, 2003).

The idea of a "goddess," of course, was a European, not Indian, conception that continued an earlier Europeanization, the "Indian queen," that beginning in the sixteenth century was often used by Europeans as a symbol of the spirit of the Indigenous "New World" (ibid.).

6. Margaret Vaughn, "Expanding Jamaica Kincaid's 'Garden of Empire' to Interpret a North Dakota Seed Catalogue," paper presented to

36th Annual Southwest/American Popular Culture Association (SWPACA) Meeting, 2015; Margaret Vaughn, "The Colonial Empire of the Garden Seed Catalog Narratives Told and Products Sold," 38th Annual Southwest/American Popular Culture Association (SWPACA) Meeting, 2017. Abstracts of both papers are available at southwestpca. org.

7. John C. Calhoun, "A Disquisition on Government and Discourse on the Constitution and Government of the United States," in *The Works of John C. Calhoun*, ed. Richard K. Kralle (New York: Appleton, 1851), briefly discussed in Grinde and Johnson, *Exemplar of Liberty*, 219.

8. Lewis Henry Morgan, *Ancient Society or Researches in the Lines of Human Progress from Savagery through Barbarism to Civilization* (New York: H. Holt, 1877), chap. 1, www.marxists.org/reference/archive/morgan-lewis/ancient-society/ch01.htm. The information that Morgan was assisted by Parker in portions of his Six Nation ethnography was supplied in a communication from historian Barbara Alice Mann, professor of humanities at the University of Toledo, and member of the Bear Clan of the Ohio Seneca. She has written extensively on Indian issues. It can also be found in Scott Michaelsen, *The Limits of Multiculturalism: Interrogating the Origins of American Anthropology* (Minneapolis: University of Minnesota Press, 1999), chap. 3.

9. Ibid., chap. 5.

10. Letter of Lewis Henry Morgan to Henry R. Schoolcraft, May 12, 1847, from the Morgan Papers at the University of Rochester, as reported in Grinde and Johansen, *Exemplar of Liberty*, 220, 301nn10–11. Schoolcraft was an ethnographer of American Indians, as well as a geographer and geologist. He was commissioned by Congress in 1846 to compile a major study of Indians, which he published as *Information Respecting the History, Condition, and Prospects of the Indian Tribes of the United States* in six volumes from 1851 to 1857. A short biography of Schoolcraft is available on Wikipedia under "Henry Schoolcraft," https://en.wikipedia.org/wiki/Henry_Schoolcraft.

11. Grinde and Johansen, *Exemplars of Liberty*, 99, 160–75, 180–82, 192–95, 211–19, 289, 295–301; Donald A. Grinde, "Iroquoian Political Concept and the Genesis of American Government," in *Indian Roots of American Democracy*, ed. Jose Barreiro (Ithaca, NY: Akwe:kon, 1992), 50, 55, 62n18; "Tammanies," Wikipedia, https://en.wikipedia.org/wiki/Tammanies; "Tammany Hall," Wikipedia, https://en.wikipedia.org/wiki/Tammany_Hall. Note that "Tamenund" was the title for the leader of a Lenape clan, who took the title as a name while serving

in that office. The Tamenund in question lived from about 1625 to around 1702.

12. Frederick Webb Hodge, ed., *Handbook of Indians North of Mexico*, Smithsonian Institution, Bureau of American Ethnology Bulletin 30 (Washington, DC: Government Publishing Office, 1911); and "Tammanies," Wikipedia, https://en.wikipedia.org/wiki/Tammanies.

13. De Witt Clinton, "Discourse Delivered before the New York Historical Society, at their Anniversary Meeting, 6th December, 1811," http://digital.library.pitt.edu/cgi-bin/t/text/pageviewer-idx?c=darltext&cc=darltext&idno=31735054852417&q1=Iroquois+Indians.&frm=framese t&view=image&seq=1, particularly 6–16. This is also briefly discussed in Grinde and Johansen, *Exemplars of Liberty*, 218–19. On DeWitt Clinton, see "Clinton, De Witt," Biographical Directory of the United States Congress, http://bioguide.congress.gov/scripts/biodisplay. pl?index=C000525; Evan Cornog, *The Birth of Empire: De Witt Clinton and the American Experience, 1769–1828* (New York: Oxford University Press, 1998); Steven E. Siry, *De Witt Clinton and the American Political Economy: Sectionalism, Politics, and Republican Ideology, 1787–1828* (New York: Peter Lang, 1990); and "DeWitt Clinton," Wikipedia, https://en.wikipedia.org/wiki/DeWitt_Clinton.

14. For example, see Bruce E. Johansen, *Debating Democracy: Native American Legacy of Freedom* (Santa Fe, NM: Clear Light, 1998); Grinde and Johansen, *Exemplars of Liberty*; Barreiro, ed., *Indian Roots of American Democracy*; Oren R. Lyons, John C. Mohawk, Vine Deloria Jr., Laurence M. Hauptman, Howard R. Berman, Donald A. Grinde Jr., Curtis G. Berkey, and Robert W. Venables, *Exiled in the Land of the Free: Democracy, Indian Nations, and the U.S. Constitution* (Santa Fe, NM: Clear Light, 1992); Donald A. Grinde Jr., *The Iroquois and the Founding of the American Nation* (San Francisco: Indian Historian, 1977); Scott L. Pratt, *Native Pragmatism: Rethinking the Roots of American Philosophy* (Bloomington: Indiana University Press, 2002); Betty Booth Donohue, *Bradford's Indian Book: Being the True Roote & Rise of American Letters as Revealed by the Native Text Embedded in* Of Plymouth Plantation (Gainesville: University of Florida Press, 2011); Jack Weatherford, *Indian Givers: How the Indians of America Transformed the World* (New York: Fawcett Columbine, 1988); and Emory Dean Keoke and Kay Marie Porterfield, *American Indian Contributions to the World* (New York: Checkmark, 2003).

15. Johansen, *Debating Democracy*, 122.

16. Keoke and Porterfield, *American Indian Contributions to the World*, 100–101; and Robert Coles, *Erik H. Erikson: The Growth of His Work* (Boston: Little, Brown, 1970).

17. Discussion of the inspiration of "two-spirit" Native roles on the LGBT movement, including misconceptions about the traditional roles by non-Natives, is in Michelle Cameron, "Two-Spirited Aboriginal People: Continuing Cultural Appropriation by Non-Aboriginal Society," *Canadian Women Studies* 24, no. 2/3 (2005): 123–27; and Mary Annette Pember, "'Two Spirit' Tradition Far from Ubiquitous among Tribes," *Rewire*, October 13, 2016, https://rewire.news/article/2016/10/13/two-spirit-tradition-far-ubiquitous-among-tribes/. Further discussion of "two-spirit" roles in American Indian societies with references is in chapter 1 of this volume.

18. The original plan was for Scott Pratt, professor of philosophy at the University of Oregon, to draft this section on the Indian roots of the American philosophy of pragmatism, with follow-up input from Stephen Sachs and other authors of this book. However, following the pragmatist concern that philosophy is to be carried out in action in arising circumstances, when major discussions of issues by students, faculty, and administration resulted both in a change in university policy and an offer for Pratt to become dean of the University of Oregon Graduate School, he accepted the position. As a result, he was unable to devote the necessary time to developing a first draft of the section. The drafting was then undertaken by Stephen Sachs, with heavy reliance on upon Pratt's research, which is often cited. Pratt was then able to respond briefly to Sachs's draft, with a helpful comment assisting in one revision. As with all parts of this book, all of the authors have had the opportunity to offer editing suggestions to the draft of the section.

19. Pratt, *Native Pragmatism*, 222–25.

20. Ibid., 229–79.

21. Lydia Maria Child, *Hobomok and other Writings on Indians*, ed. and intro. Caroline L. Karcher (New Brunswick, NJ: Rutgers University Press, 1986); discussed in Pratt, *Native Pragmatism*, 229–40.

22. Pratt, *Native Pragmatism*, 232–34.

23. On William Apess (sometimes written as Apes), see Alexander Keller Hirsch, "Agonism and Hope in William Apess's Native American Political Thought," *New Political Science* 39, no. 3 (2017); James Tully, *Public Philosophy in a New Key*, vols. 1–2 (Cambridge: Cambridge University Press, 2009); Barry O'Connell, ed., *On Our Own Ground:*

The Complete Writings of William Apess, a Pequot (Amherst: University of Massachusetts Press, 1992); Patricia Bizzell, "(Native) American Jeremiad: The 'Mixedblood' Rhetoric of William Apess," in *American Indian Rhetorics of* Survivance*: Word Medicine, Word Magic*, ed. Ernest Stromberg (Pittsburgh, PA: University of Pittsburgh Press, 2006); Barry O'Connell, ed., *A Son of the Forest and Other Writings* (Amherst: University of Massachusetts Press, 1997); and "William Apess," Wikipedia, https://en.wikipedia.org/wiki/William_Apess. Project Guttenberg and the Internet Archives offer writings by Apess online.

24. William Apess, "Indian Nullification," in *On Our Own Ground*, 200–201.

25. Hirsch, "Agonism and Hope," 384. For influence on Child, see Laura Mielke, *Moving Encounters: Sympathy and the Indian Question in Antebellum Literature* (Amherst: University of Massachusetts Press, 2008). For influence on Thoreau and Douglass, see Rene Bergland, *The National Uncanny: Indian Ghosts and American Subjects* (Hanover, NH: Dartmouth College Press, 2000), 114–16. For influence on Melville, see Samuel Otter, *Melville's Anatomies* (Berkeley: University of California Press, 1999).

26. Ma-ka-tai-me-she-kia-kiak, known as Black Hawk, lived from 1767 to 1838. He was a band leader and warrior of the Sauk Nation in what is now the US Midwest. With the aid of a newspaper reporter and an editor, his autobiography was published, Black Hawk, *Autobiography of Ma-Ka-Tai-Me-She-Kia-Kiak, or Black Hawk, Embracing the Traditions of His Nation, Various Wars in Which He Has Been Engaged, and His Account of the Cause and General History of the Black Hawk War of 1832* (Charleston, SC: CreateSpace Independent, 2015). Also see Roger L. Nichols, *Black Hawk and the Warrior's Path* (Arlington Heights, IL: Harlan Davidson, 1992); and "Black Hawk (Sauk Leader)," Wikipedia, https://en.wikipedia.org/wiki/Black_Hawk_(Sauk_leader)#Early_autobiography_by_Native_American.

27. On Elias Boudinot, John Ross, and other influential Cherokee, see Samuel Carter, *Cherokee Sunset* (Garden City, NY: Doubleday, 1976); Thurman Wilkins, *Cherokee Tragedy: The Story of the Ridge Family and the Decimation of a People* (London: Macmillan, 1970); Edward Everett Dale, *Cherokee Cavaliers: Forty Years of Cherokee History as Told in the Correspondences of the Ridge-Watie-Boudinot Family* (Norman: University of Oklahoma Press, 1939); "Elias Boudinot (Cherokee)," Wikipedia, https://en.wikipedia.org/wiki/Elias_Boudinot_(Cherokee). *The Cherokee Phoenix*, 1828 to the present, www.cherokeephoenix.org. Elias Boudinot, "An Address to the Whites: Speech Delivered in the First

Presbyterian Church, Philadelphia, May 26, 1826," Excerpts, National Humanities Center, http://nationalhumanitiescenter.org/pds/triumphnationalism/expansion/text3/addresswhites.pdf.

28. On George Copway, *Kah-Ge-Ga-Gah-Bowh*, see Donald B. Smith, Mississauga Portraits (Toronto, ON: University of Toronto Press, 2013); George Copway, *The Life, History, and Travels of Kah-ge-ga-gah-bowh (George Copway), a Young Indian Chief of the Ojebwa Nation, a Convert to the Christian Faith, and a Missionary to His People for Twelve Years* (Albany, NY: P. Weed and Parsons, 1847), http://fax.libs.uga.edu/E99xC6xC73x1846/; and "George Copway," Wikipedia, https://en.wikipedia.org/wiki/George_Copway.

29. Pratt, *Native Pragmatism*, 240–44.

30. Roger Williams, *A Key into the Language of America* [1643], ed. John J. Teunissen and Evelyn J. Hinz (Detroit, MI: Wayne State Press, 1973), and discussed in Pratt, *Native Pragmatism*, 85, 96–98, 100–105, 111, 119, 241. Sedgwick's reading of *Key* is discussed by Pratt, *Native Pragmatism*, 240–41.

31. Catherine Maria Sedgwick, *Hope Leslie: Or Early Times in the Massachusetts*, ed. Mary Kelly (New Brunswick, NJ: Rutgers University Press, 1987), discussed by Pratt, *Native Pragmatism*, 241.

32. The "logic of home," as an element of place or diversity, is developed in Pratt, *Native Pragmatism*, chap. 10 ("Logic of Home"), particularly with reference to Child and Sedgwick. The honoring of diversity, arising from Native tradition, of these two, and some other authors, is shown in chap. 12 ("Feminism and Pragmatism") to be a major force in the movements opposing Indian relocation and slavery, as well as in the activism for the emancipation of women.

33. Philip Gould, *Covenant and Republic: Historical Romance and the Politics of Puritanism* (Cambridge: Cambridge University Press, 1996), discussed by Pratt, *Native Pragmatism*, 240.

34. Pratt, *Native Pragmatism*, 245. Wollstonecraft's role.

35. Eleanor Flexner, *Mary Wollstonecraft: A Biography* (New York: Coward, McCann, and Geoghegan, 1972); Gary Kelly, *Revolutionary Feminism: The Mind and Career of Mary Wollstonecraft* (New York: St. Martin's, 1992); and Nancy Tuana, *The Less Noble Sex: Scientific, Religious, and Philosophical Conceptions of Women's Nature* (Bloomington: University of Indiana Press, 1993).

36. Mary Wollstonecraft, *The Vindications: The Rights of Men and the Rights of Woman*, ed. D. L. Macdonald and Kathleen Scherf (Toronto: Broadview, 1997).

37. Among others, see Celia Morris Eckhardt, *Fanny Wright: Rebel in America* (Cambridge, MA: Harvard University Press, 1984); Amos Gilbeet, *Memoir of Frances Wright, the Pioneer Woman in the Cause of Human Rights* (Cincinnati, OH: Longley Brothers, 1855); and Helen Horowitz, *Rereading Sex: Battles over Sexual Knowledge and Suppression in Nineteenth-Century America* (New York: Alfred A. Knopf, 2002).

38. Frances Wright, *Views of Society and Manners in America* (London: Longman, Hurst, Rees, Orme, and Brown, 1821), https://books.google.com/books?id=w9QAAAAAYAAJ&printsec=frontcover&source=gbs_ge_summary_r&cad=0#v=onepage&q&f=false.

39. Among the huge number of writings on the history of the antislavery movement are Brycchan Carey, *From Peace to Freedom: Quaker Rhetoric and the Birth of American Antislavery, 1657–1761* (New Haven, CT: Yale University Press, 2012); Lydia Maria Child, *An Appeal in Favor of That Class of Americans Called Africans* (Boston: Allen and Ticknor, 1833); Francis D. Cogliano, *Thomas Jefferson: Reputation and Legacy* (Edinburgh: Edinburgh University Press, 2006); Allen Pell Crawford, *Twilight at Monticello: The Final Years of Thomas Jefferson* (New York: Random House, 2008); David Brion Davis, *Inhuman Bondage: The Rise and Fall of Slavery in the New World* (Oxford: Oxford University Press, 2006); John Craig Hammond and Matthew Mason, eds., *Contesting Slavery: The Politics of Bondage and Freedom in the New American Nation* (Charlottesville: University of Virginia Press, 2011); Lewis Perry and Michael Fellman, eds., *Antislavery Reconsidered: New Perspectives on the Abolitionists* (Baton Rouge: Louisiana State University Press, 1979); Michael D. Pierson, *Free Hearts and Free Homes: Gender and American Antislavery Politics* (Chapel Hill: University of North Carolina Press, 2003); Beth A. Salerno, *Sister Societies: Women's Antislavery Organizations in Antebellum America* (DeKalb: Northern Illinois University Press, 2005); and Anna M. Speicher, *The Religious World of Antislavery Women: Spirituality in the Lives of Five Abolitionist Lecturers* (Syracuse, NY: Syracuse University Press, 2000).

40. The First Great Awakening was an evangelical and revitalization movement that swept Protestant Europe and British America in the 1730s and 1740s, leaving a permanent impact on American Protestantism. It involved a shift from sacramental ritual and hierarchy to individual personal experience focused on finding a deep personal revelation of salvation through Jesus Christ. This made Christianity intensely personal to the average person by fostering a deep sense of spiritual conviction and redemption, and by encouraging introspection and

a commitment to a new standard of personal morality. See Thomas S. Kidd, *The Great Awakening: The Roots of Evangelical Christianity in Colonial America* (New Haven, CT: Yale University Press, 2009). This democratizing development moving away from dogma to personal experience is quite consistent with Indigenous ways, but whether, and if so to what extent, involved any direct or indirect Native influence is beyond the information available to this author.

41. John Locke, *The Second Treatise on Government* (Buffalo, NY: Prometheus, 1986), chap. 4, ("Of Slavery"), 14n1, states, "The natural liberty of man is to be free from any superior power on earth, and not to be under the will or legislative authority of man, but to have only the law of Nature for his rule. The liberty of man in society is to be under no other legislative power but that established by consent in the commonwealth, nor under the dominion of any will, or restraint of any law, but what that legislative shall enact according to the trust put in it." Locke goes on to say, with supporting examples, that the Bible shows that the ancient Jews did not approve slavery, though they allowed "drudgery": a labor contract to work for a limited period time in return for some good. This was a common practice in his time, of people buying their passage from England to America by agreeing to work for a number of years in the colony to which they emigrated as indentured servants. At first, Africans imported to the American colonies as slaves were treated as indentured servants, earning their freedom by working for their master for a period of years. Locke was himself connected to this "drudgery" through his investment in the East India Company, which participated in the slave trade. Unlike indentured servitude in return for passage to America, the slavery of Africans was never voluntary, and the opportunity to earn one's freedom through working for a number of years soon ended as a widespread practice.

42. The references in the US Constitution on slavery are Article 1, Section 2: "Representatives and direct Taxes shall be apportioned among the several States which may be included within this Union, according to their respective Numbers, which shall be determined by adding to the whole Number of free Persons, including those bound to Service for a Term of Years, and excluding Indians not taxed, three fifths of all other Persons"; and Article 1, Section 9: "Migration or importation of such persons as any of the states now existing shall see proper to admit, shall not be prohibited by Congress prior to the Year one thousand eight hundred and eight, but a tax or duty may be imposed on such importation, not exceeding ten dollars for each person." The

discussion of slavery at the Constitutional Convention is included in Max Farrand, *The Records of the Federal Convention of 1787*, 3 vols. (New Haven, CT: Yale University Press, 1911), http://oll.libertyfund.org/titles/farrand-the-records-of-the-federal-convention-of-1787-3vols.

43. On late-eighteenth-century US political leaders who freed their slaves, see Stephen E. Ambrose, "Founding Fathers and Slave Holders," *Smithsonian*, November 2002, www.smithsonianmag.com/history/founding-fathers-and-slaveholders-72262393/; "The Founding Fathers and Slavery," *Encyclopedia Britannica*, www.britannica.com/topic/The-Founding-Fathers-and-Slavery-1269536; Bruce Chadwick, *General and Mrs. Washington: The Untold Story of a Marriage and a Revolution* (Naperville, IL: Sourcebooks, 2007), 331; Cogliano, *Thomas Jefferson: Reputation and Legacy*; and Crawford, *Twilight at Monticello*.

44. On the invention of the cotton gin and its impact, see Angela Lakwate, *Inventing the Cotton Gin: Machine and Myth in Antebellum America* (Baltimore: Johns Hopkins University Press, 2003).

45. Quoted in Julie Roy Jeffrey, *The Great Silent Army of Abolitionism* (Chapel Hill: University of North Carolina Press, 1998), 1.

46. Child, *An Appeal in Favor of that Class of Americans Called Africans*.

47. Ralph Waldo Emerson, *Selected Essays, Lectures, and Poems*, ed. Robert D. Richardson Jr. (New York: Bantam, 1990), "Forward".

48. Pratt, *Native Pragmatism*, 213–15. For a longer consideration of the Indian impact on the development of Franklin's pragmatism, see the various discussions of Franklin in *Native Pragmatism*.

49. Ralph Waldo Emerson, *Journals of Ralph Waldo Emerson*, ed. Edward Waldo Emerson, vol. 1 (Boston and New York: Houghton Mifflin, 1909), 375–77, quoted in Pratt, *Native Pragmatism*, 214. For more on Emerson's interest in Franklin, see Jesse Bier, "Weberism, Franklin, and the Transcendental Style," *New England Quarterly* 43 (1970): 179–92; William L. Hedges, "From Franklin to Emerson," in *The Oldest Revolutionary: Essays on Benjamin Franklin*, ed. A. Leo Lemay (Philadelphia: University of Pennsylvania Press, 1976).

50. Ralph Waldo Emerson, "Letter to Martin Van Buren President of the United States, 1836," http://www.cherokee.org/AboutTheNation/History/TrailofTears/RalphWaldoEmersonsLetter.aspx:

Sir:

The seat you fill places you in a relation of credit and nearness to every citizen. By right and natural position, every citizen is your friend. Before any acts contrary to his own judgment or interest have repelled the affections of any man, each may look with trust and living anticipation to your government. Each has the highest right to call your attention to such subjects as are of a public nature, and properly belong to the chief magistrate; and the good magistrate will feel a joy in meeting such confidence. In this belief and at the instance of a few of my friends and neighbors, I crave of your patience a short hearing for their sentiments and my own: and the circumstances that my name will be utterly unknown to you will only give the fairer chance to your equitable construction of what I have to say.

Sir, my communication respects the sinister rumors that fill this part of the country concerning the Cherokee people. The interest always felt in the aboriginal population—an interest naturally growing as that decays—has been heightened in regard to this tribe. Even in our distant State some good rumor of their worth and civility has arrived. We have learned with joy their improvement in the social arts. We have read their newspapers. We have seen some of them in our schools and colleges. In common with the great body of the American people, we have witnessed with sympathy the painful labors of these red men to redeem their own race from the doom of eternal inferiority, and to borrow and domesticate in the tribe the arts and customs of the Caucasian race. And notwithstanding the unaccountable apathy with which of late years the Indians have been sometimes abandoned to their enemies, it is not to be doubted that it is the good pleasure and the understanding of all humane persons in the Republic, of the men and the matrons sitting in the thriving independent families all over the land, that they shall be duly cared for; that they shall taste justice and love from all to whom we have delegated the office of dealing with them.

The newspapers now inform us that, in December, 1835, a treaty contracting for the exchange of all the Cherokee territory was pretended to be made by an agent on the part of the United States with some persons appearing on the part of the Cherokees; that the fact afterwards transpired that these deputies did by no means represent the will of the nation; and that, out of eighteen thousand souls composing the nation, fifteen thousand six hundred and sixty-eight have protested against the so-called treaty. It now appears that the government of the United States choose to hold the Cherokees to this sham treaty, and are proceeding to execute the same. Almost the entire Cherokee Nation stand up and say, "This is not our act. Behold us. Here are we. Do not mistake that handful of deserters for us;" and the American President and the Cabinet, the Senate and the House of Representatives, neither hear these men nor see them, and are contracting to put this active nation into carts and boats, and to drag them over mountains and rivers to a wilderness at a vast distance beyond the Mississippi. As a paper purporting to be an army order fixes a month from this day as the hour for this doleful removal.

In the name of God, sir, we ask you if this be so. Do the newspapers rightly inform us? Man and women with pale and perplexed faces meet one another in the streets and churches here, and ask if this be so. We have inquired if this be a gross misrepresentation from the party opposed to the government and anxious to blacken it with the people. We have looked at the newspapers of different parties and find a horrid confirmation of the tale. We are slow to believe it. We hoped the Indians were misinformed, and that their remonstrance was premature, and will turn out to be a needless act of terror.

The piety, the principle that is left in the United States, if only in its coarsest form, a regard to the speech of men, forbid us to entertain it as a fact. Such a dereliction of all faith and virtue, such a denial of justice, and such deafness to screams for mercy were never heard of in times of peace and in the dealing of a nation with its own allies and wards, since the earth was made. Sir, does this government think that the people of the United States are become savage and mad? From their mind are the sentiments of love and a good nature wiped clean out? The soul of man, the justice, the mercy that is the heart in all men from Maine to Georgia, does abhor this business.

In speaking thus the sentiments of my neighbors and my own, perhaps I overstep the bounds of decorum. But would it not be a higher indecorum coldly to argue a matter like this? We only state the fact that a crime is projected that confounds our understanding by its magnitude, a crime that really deprives us as well as the Cherokees of a country for how could we call the conspiracy that should crush these poor Indians our government, or the land that was cursed by their parting and dying imprecations our country, any more? You, sir, will bring down that renowned chair in which you sit into infamy if your seal is set to this instrument of perfidy; and the name of this nation, hitherto the sweet omen of religion and liberty, will stink to the world.

You will not do us the injustice of connecting this remonstrance with any sectional and party feeling. It is in our hearts the simplest commandment of brotherly love. We will not have this great and solemn claim upon national and human justice huddled aside under the flimsy plea of its being a party act. Sir, to us the questions upon which the government and the people have been agitated during the past year, touching the prostration of the currency and of trade, seem but motes in comparison. These hard times, it is true, have brought the discussion home to every farmhouse and poor man's house in this town; but it is the chirping of grasshoppers beside the immortal question whether justice shall be done by the race of civilized to the race of savage man, whether all the attributes of reason, of civility, of justice, and even of mercy, shall be put off by the American people, and so vast an outrage upon the Cherokee Nation and upon human nature shall be consummated.

One circumstance lessens the reluctance with which I intrude at this time on your attention my conviction that the government ought to be admonished of a new historical fact, which the discussion of this question has disclosed, namely, that there exists in a great part of the Northern people a gloomy diffidence in the moral character of the government.

On the broaching of this question, a general expression of despondency, of disbelief that any good will accrue from a remonstrance on an act of fraud and robbery, appeared in those men to whom we naturally turn for aid and counsel. Will the American government steal? Will it lie? Will it kill?—We ask triumphantly. Our counselors and old statesmen here say that ten years ago they would have staked their lives on the affirmation that the proposed Indian measures could not be executed; that the unanimous country would put them down. And now the steps of this crime follow each other so fast, at such fatally quick time, that the millions of virtuous citizens, whose agents the government are, have no place to interpose, and must shut their eyes until the last howl and wailing of these tormented villages and tribes shall afflict the ear of the world.

I will not hide from you, as an indication of the alarming distrust, that a letter addressed as mine is, and suggesting to the mind of the Executive the plain obligations of man, has a burlesque character in the apprehensions of some of my friends. I, sir, will not beforehand treat you with the contumely of this distrust. I will at least state to you this fact, and show you how plain and humane people, whose love would be honor, regard the policy of the government, and what injurious inferences they draw as to the minds of the governors. A man with your experience in affairs must have seen cause to appreciate the futility of opposition to the moral sentiment. However feeble the sufferer and however great the oppressor, it is in the nature of things that the blow should recoil upon the aggressor. For God is in the sentiment, and it cannot be withstood. The potentate and the people perish before it; but with it, and its executor, they are omnipotent.

I write thus, sir, to inform you of the state of mind these Indian tidings have awakened here, and to pray with one voice more that you, whose hands are strong with the delegated power of fifteen millions of men, will avert with that might the terrific injury which threatens the Cherokee tribe.

With great respect, sir, I am your fellow citizen,
Ralph Waldo Emerson

51. Pratt, *Native Pragmatism*, 215n22.

52. Emerson, *Selected Essays, Lectures, and Poems*, 5. Richardson's "forward" briefly discusses influences upon Emerson's thinking, particularly 4–6.

53. Ibid., 4–11.

54. Ibid., 4–5.

55. Ibid., 5––6.

56. Ibid., 15.

57. Ibid., 17–18.

58. Ibid., 39.

59. Ibid., 50.

60. Ibid., 37.

61. Ibid., 54.

62. On Thoreau, see "Thoreau Reader: Annotated Works of Henry David Thoreau," Thoreau Reader, A Project in Cooperation with the Thoreau Society, http://thoreau.eserver.org; Robert D. Richardson Jr., *Henry Thoreau: A Life of the Mind* (Berkeley: University of California Press, 1986); Walter Harding, *The Days of Henry Thoreau: A Biography* (New York: Alfred A. Knopf, 1910; reprint, Mineola, NY: Dover Press, 1965); Henry Seidel Canby, *Thoreau* (Boston: Houghton Mifflin, 1939); Sandra H. Petrulionis, ed., *Thoreau in His Own Time: A Biographical Chronicle of His Life, Drawn from Recollections, Memoirs, and Interviews by Friends and Associates* (Iowa City: Iowa University Press, 2012); Richard J. Schneider, "Life and Legacy: Thoreau's Life," Thoreau Society, http://thoreausociety.org/life-legacy; and "Henry David Thoreau: Philosopher, Journalist, Poet (1817–1862)," Biography.com, www.biography.com/people/henry-david-thoreau-9506784.

63. Ralph Waldo Emerson's Eulogy of May 9th, 1862. Published in the *Atlantic Monthly*, 1862, www.wsfcs.k12.nc.us/cms/lib/NC01001395/Centricity/ModuleInstance/17580/Emersons_Eulogy_for_Thoreau.pdf.

64. Bradley P. Dean, "A Compilation of Indian References," with notes by Dave Bonney, sent by Dean to Connie Baxter Marlow via email 2005, who shared them via email with Stephen Sachs on January 7, 2014. Marlow noted in the email to Sachs that "June 2005 Brad joined Connie in Aspen, Colorado for a seminar entitled: 'Thoreau and the Evolution of the American Mind: The Next Step. A Tapestry of Ideas.' This seminar was filmed and Connie has a transcript of Brad's presentations. For more information on the seminar go to www.TheAmericanEvolution.com."

"A Compilation of Indian References" quotes Thoreau's references to Indians in his writings as follows:

Section I: Journals (517 entries), p. 1.
Section II: *A Week on the Concord and Merrimack Rivers* (51 entries), p. 96.
Section III: *Walden* (51 entries), p. 110.
Section IV: *The Maine Woods* (325 entries), p. 117.
Section V: *Cape Cod* (28 entries), p. 172.
Section VI: *The Dispersion of Seeds* (8 entries), p. 177.
Section VII: *Wild Fruits* (45 entries), p. 178.
Section VIII: Thoreau's Essays (54 entries), p. 186.
Section IX: Thoreau's Poems (6 entries), p. 195.
Section X: Early Essays from: Princeton's *Early Essays and Miscellanies* (7 entries), p. 197.

65. Dean, "A Compilation of Indian References" [Journal 3710–12, 2 references], October 29, 1837; *Early Essays and Miscellanies*, vol. 1, 8–9, "The Arrowhead."

66. Dean, "A Compilation of Indian References" [Journal 4007–12_PEJ, 4 references], December 16, 1840; *Early Essays and Miscellanies*, vol. 1, 205.

67. Dean, "A Compilation of Indian References" [Journal 3805–06, 1 reference], May 10, 1838; *Early Essays and Miscellanies*, vol. 1, 46.

68. Dean, "A Compilation of Indian References" [Journal 5309, 34 references], September 17, 1853 (omitted from the 1906 edition).

69. Per Dean, "Long Book Fall 1842–March, 1846" [Journal PEJ2-001-060, 9 references], 1842–1844; *Early Essays and Miscellanies*, vol. 2, 38–40.

70. Per Dean, "A Compilation of Indian References" [Journal 4201-06_PEJ, 6 references], April 26, 1841; *Early Essays and Miscellanies*, vol. 1, 304.

71. Per Dean, "Long Book Fall 1842–March, 1846, [Journal PEJ2-061-104, 6 references], 1842–1844 [after August 1, 1844]; *Early Essays and Miscellanies*, vol. 2, 100–101.

72. Per Dean, "A Compilation of Indian References" [Journal 5210, 2 references], October 25, 1852; *Early Essays and Miscellanies*, vol. 5, 385.

73. In Dean, sect. X, "A Compilation of Indian References in Thoreau's Early Essays" [7 entries], June 2, 1837; *Early Essays and Miscellanies*, 109–10.

74. Ibid., 110.

75. Walter Harding, "Live Your Own Life," *Geneseo Summer Compass*, June 4, 1984.

76. Robert Sattelmeyer, *Thoreau's Reading: A Study in Intellectual History with Bibliographical Catalogue* (Princeton, NJ: Princeton University Press, 1988), chap. 2.

77. Randall Conrad, "Machine in the Wetland: Re-imagining Thoreau's Plumbago-Grinder," *Thoreau Society Bulletin* (Fall 2005).

78. Thoreau, "Where I Lived, and What I Lived For," in *Walden*, as quoted in "Henry David Thoreau," Wikipedia, https://en.wikipedia.org/wiki/Henry_David_Thoreau.

79. Lawrence Rosenwald, "The Theory, Practice, and Influence of Thoreau's Civil Disobedience," in *A Historical Guide to Henry David Thoreau*, ed. William Cain (New York: Oxford University Press, 2000). *Thoreau* used with the author's permission, http://thoreau.eserver.org/theory.html#n1 (unfortunately this webpage no longer works).

80. Henry David Thoreau, "Resistance to Government," in *Aesthetic Papers*, ed. Elizabeth P. Peabody (Boston: G. P. Putnam, 1849), http://commons.digitalthoreau.org/civil/.

81. Rosenwald, "The Theory, Practice, and Influence of Thoreau's Civil Disobedience," 29, pt. 3, used with the author's permission.

82. Martin Luther King, *The Autobiography of Martin King, Jr.*, ed. Clayborne Carson (New York: Warner, 1998), chaps. 2, 13.

83. Per Dean, "A Plea for Captain John Brown" (*Early Essays and Miscellanies*, 124–25).

84. Ibid., 133.

85. Henry David Thoreau, *Autumnal Tints* [1862] (Bedford, MA: Applewood, 1992), originally published just after Thoreau's death; Henry David Thoreau, *Wild Apples* (Bedford, MA: Applewood, 1992), which first appeared in the *Atlantic Monthly* in November 1862; and Henry David Thoreau, *Walking* (Bedford, MA: Applewood, 1992). All of these works, as well as Thoreau's *Walden* and others, are available from the Thoreau Society, http://www.shopatwaldenpond.org/By_Thoreau_s/1.htm.

86. Catharine Beecher, *Treatise on Domestic Economy* (New York: Harper, 1850). See the discussion in Pratt, *Native Pragmatism*, 277–79.

87. Catharine E. Beecher and Harriet Beecher Stowe, *The American Woman's Home* (New York: J. B. Ford, 1869), discussed in Pratt, *Native Pragmatism*, 278–79.

88. Susan Cheever, *Louisa May Alcott: A Personal Biography* (New York: Simon and Schuster, 2011); John Matteson, *Eden's Outcasts: The Story of Louisa May Alcott and Her Father* (New York: W. W. Norton, 2007); Elaine Showalter, *Alternative Alcott* (New Brunswick, NJ: Rutgers University Press, 1988); "Louisa May Alcott: The Woman behind *Little Women*, the Alcotts," Nancy Porter Productions, www.alcottfilm.com/louisa-may-alcott/life/; Rebecca Beatrice Brooks, "Louisa May Alcott: The First Woman to Vote in Concord," History of Massachusetts, September 19, 2011, http://historyofmassachusetts.org/louisa-may-alcott-the-first-woman-registered-to-vote-in-concord/; "Louisa May Alcott," Wikipedia, https://en.wikipedia.org/wiki/Louisa_May_Alcott; and Pratt, *Native Pragmatism*, 279.

89. Louisa May Alcott, *Hospital Sketches* (Boston: James Redpath, 1863).

90. Pratt, *Native Pragmatism*, 279.

91. Louisa May Alcott, *Work: A Story of Experience* (Boston: Roberts, 1873); and Pratt, *Native Pragmatism*, 279.

92. Charlotte Perkins Gilman, *The Living of Charlotte Perkins Gilman: An Autobiography* (New York: D. Appleton-Century, 1935; reprint, New York: Arno, 1972; reprint, New York: Harper & Row, 1975); Charlotte (Anna) Perkins (Stetson) Gilman, "Charlotte (Anna) Perkins (Stetson) Gilman," Contemporary Authors Online; Denise D. Knight, *The Diaries of Charlotte Perkins Gilman* (Charlottesville, VA: University Press of Virginia: 1994); "Charlotte Perkins Gilman," Wikipedia, https://en.wikipedia.org/wiki/Charlotte_Perkins_Gilman; and Pratt, *Native Pragmatism*, 279–80.

93. Charlotte Perkins Gilman, *Women and Economics: A Study of the Economic Relation between Men and Women as a Factor in Social Evolution* (Boston: Small, Maynard, 1898). See the discussion of it in Pratt, *Native Pragmatism*, 279–80.

94. Perkins Gilman, *Women and Economics*, 220, quoted in Pratt, *Native Pragmatism*, 280.

95. Victoria Bissell Brown, *The Education of Jane Addams* (Philadelphia: University of Pennsylvania Press, 2004); Allen F. Davis, *American Heroine: The Life and Legend of Jane Addams* (Oxford: Oxford University Press, 1973); Gioia Diliberto, *A Useful Woman: The Early Life of Jane Addams* (New York: Scribner, 1999); John C. Farrell, *Beloved Lady: A History of Jane Addams' Ideas on Reform and Peace* (Baltimore, MD: Johns Hopkins University Press, 1967); Katherine Joslin, *Jane Addams: A Writer's Life* (Urbana: University of Illinois Press, 2004); Louise Knight, *Citizen: Jane Addams and the Struggle for Democracy* (Chicago: University of Chicago Press, 2005); Louise Knight, *Jane Addams: Spirit*

in Action for Democracy (New York: W. W. Norton, 2010); James Weber Linn, *Jane Addams: A Biography* (Urbana: University of Illinois Press, 2000); Jean Bethke Elshtain, *Jane Addams and the Dream of American Democracy* (New York: Basic, 2002); Maurice Hamington and Celia Bardwell-Jones, eds., *Contemporary Feminist Pragmatism* (London: Routledge, 2012); Maurice Hamington, *Embodied Care: Jane Addams, Maurice Merleau-Ponty, and Feminist Ethics* (Urbana: University of Illinois Press, 2004); Maurice Hamington, *The Social Philosophy of Jane Addams* (Urbana: University of Illinois Press, 2009); Maurice Hamington, ed., *Feminist Interpretations of Jane Addams* (University Park: Pennsylvania State University Press, 2010); Christopher Lasch, *The Social Thought of Jane Addams* (Indianapolis, IN: Bobbs-Merrill, 1965); Charlene Haddock Seigfried, *Pragmatism and Feminism: Reweaving the Social Fabric* (Chicago: University of Chicago Press, 1996); Mary Jo Deegan, "Jane Addams, the Hull-House School of Sociology, and Social Justice, 1892 to 1935," *Humanity and Society* 37, no. 3 (2013): 248–58; and "Jane Addams," *Stanford Encyclopedia of Philosophy*, June 7, 2006 (substantive revision May 23, 2018), https:// plato.stanford.edu/entries/addams-jane/#Bib. "Jane Addams," Wikipedia, https://en.wikipedia.org/wiki/Jane_Addams, includes an extensive list of Addams's writings, in many instances with links to them online. Pratt, *Native Pragmatism*, 280–84.

96. Jane Addams, *Democracy and Social Ethics* (New York: MacMillan, 1902; reprint, Urbana: University of Illinois Press, 2002); discussed in Pratt, *Native Pragmatism*, 280–81.

97. Jane Addams, *Twenty Years at Hull House: With Autobiographical Notes by Jane Addams* (New York: Signet Classics, 1981).

98. Pratt, *Native Pragmatism*, 282n13. Pratt points out that little research has been published on this interaction, or on some of those involved in the Pan-Indian movement of that era. There is some discussion of it in the introduction to part II of this volume.

99. Davis, *American Heroine*, 96–97, quoted in Pratt, *Native Pragmatism*, 282–83.

100. Robert W. Venables, *Conquest of a Continent, 1492–1783*, vol. 1 of *American Indian History: Five Centuries of Conflict and Coexistence* (Santa Fe, NM: Clear Light, 2004), 205–20.

101. William G. McLoughlin, *After the Trail of Tears: The Cherokee's Struggle for Sovereignty, 1839–1880* (Chapel Hill: University of North Carolina Press, 2014); Kevin Mulroy, *The Seminole Freedmen: A History* (Norman: University of Oklahoma Press, 2007); and Tiya Miles, *Ties That Bind:*

The Story of an Afro-Cherokee Family in Slavery and Freedom, 2nd ed. (Oakland: University of California Press, 2015).

102. W. E. B. Du Bois, "On the Conservation of Race," WEBDubois.org, http://www.webdubois.org/dbConsrvOfRaces.html.

103. Erin McKenna and Scott L. Pratt, *American Philosophy: From Wounded Knee to the Present* (New York: Bloomsbury, 2015), 117.

104. Ibid., 24, 25, 30, 31, 32, and chap. 13.

105, Cornell West, *Race Matters* (Boston: Beacon, 1993), 103, quoted in McKenna and Pratt, *American Philosophy*, 364. For more on West, see McKenna and Pratt, *American Philosophy*, 4, 5, 6, 213, 258–60, 275, 303, 336, 343, 345, 349, 355, 359, 363–68, 371–72, 379–81, 394, 406–7.

106. McKenna and Pratt, *American Philosophy*, 362.

107. Cornell West, *The American Evasion of Philosophy: A Genealogy of Pragmatism* (Madison: University of Wisconsin Press, 1989).

108. West, *American Evasion of Philosophy*, 239, quoted in McKenna and Pratt, *American Philosophy*, 383.

109. Pratt, *Native Pragmatism*, chap. 2 ("American Pragmatism") summarizes and shows the main principles of the development of classical pragmatism, indicating the main differences in approaching those principles among the three pragmatists.

110. John Dewey, *Reconstruction in Philosophy* [1948], in *The Later Works: 1925–1953*, ed. J. Boydston, vol. 12 (Carbondale: University of Illinois Press, 1981–90), 256, quoted in Pratt, *Native Pragmatism*, 17.

111. John Dewey, *Philosophy* [1934], in *The Later Works*, vols. 12, 29, quoted in Pratt, *Native Pragmatism*, 17.

112. Pratt, *Native Pragmatism*, 85, and chap. 2.

113. Charles Sanders Peirce, "How to Make Our Ideas Clear," in *The Essential Peirce*, eds. Nathan Houser and Christian Kloesel, vol. 1 (Bloomington: University of Indiana Press, 1992), 132, quoted in Pratt, *Native Pragmatism*, 20.

114. William James, *The Writings of William James*, ed. J. J. McDermott (New York: Random House, 1967), 349, quoted in Pratt, *Native Pragmatism*, 20.

115. John Dewey, *The Logic of Enquiry* [1938], in *The Later Works*, vols. 12, 31, quoted in Pratt, *Native Pragmatism*, 24.

116. William James, *Pragmatism: A New Name for Some Old Ways of Thinking and Meaning of Truth; A Sequel to Pragmatism* (Cambridge, MA: Harvard University Press, 1975), quoted in Pratt, *Native Pragmatism*, 25.

117. Peirce, *The Essential Peirce*, vol. 1, p. 310, quoted in Pratt, *Native Pragmatism*, 26.

118. Ibid., 331, quoted in Pratt, *American Philosophy*, 26.

119. John Dewey, *The Quest for Certainty* [1929], in *The Later Works*, vol. 2, pp. 176–77, quoted in Pratt, *American Philosophy*, 27.

120. Dewey, *The Quest for Certainty*, 157, quoted in Pratt, *American Philosophy*, 27.

121. Charles Sanders Peirce, "Some Consequences of Four Incapacities," in *The Essential Peirce*, vol. 1, pp. 54–55, quoted in Pratt, *American Philosophy*, 28.

122. William James, *The Principles of Psychology* [1890] (New York: Dover, 1950), 294, quoted in Pratt, *American Philosophy*, 29.

123. John Dewey, *Logic: The Theory of Enquiry*, in *The Later Works*, vol. 12, p. 52, quoted in Pratt, *American Philosophy*, 30.

124. Pratt, *American Philosophy*, 30–31.

125. John Dewey, *Democracy and Education*, in *The Middle Works: 1899–1924*, ed. Jo Ann Boydston, vol. 4 (Carbondale: University of Illinois Press, 1976–83), 182, quoted in Pratt, *American Philosophy*, 31.

126. Pratt, *American Philosophy*, 32–33.

127. Charles Sanders Peirce, "How to Make Our Ideas Clear," in *The Essential Peirce*, vol. 2 (Bloomington: University of Indiana Press, 1998), 373–74, discussed with some quotes in Pratt, *Native Pragmatism*, 32–33.

128. Peirce, *The Essential Peirce*, vol. 1, p. 362, discussed in Pratt, *Native Pragmatism*, 32.

129. Ibid., 354, quoted in Pratt, *Native Pragmatism*, 32–33.

130. William James, *The Varieties of Religious Experience* (New York: Longmans, Green, 1902), 508.

131. James, *Pragmatism: A New Name*, 138.

132. John Dewey, *Experience and Nature*, in *The Later Works*, vol. 1, p. 210, quoted in Pratt, *American Philosophy*, 35.

133. John Dewey, *The Logic of Enquiry* [1938], in *The Later Works*, vol. 12, p. 19, quoted in Pratt, *American Philosophy*, 36.

134. John Dewey, *Ethics*, rev. ed. [1932], in *The Later Works*, vol. 7, p. 305, quoted in Pratt, *American Philosophy*, 36.

135. Ibid.

136. On William James, see McKenna and Pratt, *American Philosophy*, xxi–xiv, 2–3, 5, 50–53, 66, 69, 72, 74, 82, 90, 102–8, 116–17, 122–23, 132–33, 137, 140–43, 165, 167, 170, 187–92, 199, 202, 207, 212, 243, 260, 263–64, 267–68, 287, 306, 315, 328 330–33, 336, 338–46, 353, 356, 358–60, 364, 370–72, 275, 383–84, 390, 401–6, and chap. 7; Pratt, *Native Pragmatism*, xv, 6–7, 9–10, 20–23, 25–26, 28–30, 33–35, 213, 215; Bruce Wilshire, *The Primal Roots of American Philosophy*

(University Park: Pennsylvania State University Press, 2000), ix–x, 13, 20–22, 142–43, 160, 164, 181, 191–206, 209, and chaps. 3, 4, 5; James Sloan Allen, *William James on Habit, Will, Truth, and the Meaning of Life* (Savannah, GA: Frederic C. Beil, 2014); Wesley Cooper, *The Unity of William James's Thought* (Nashville, TN, Vanderbilt University Press, 2002); Howard M. Feinstein, *Becoming William James* (Ithaca, NY: Cornell University Press, 1984); Gerald E. Myers, *William James: His Life and Thought* (New Haven, CT: Yale University Press, 1986); Robert D. Richardson, ed., *The Heart of William James* (Cambridge, MA: Harvard University Press, 2010); Josiah Royce, *William James and Other Essays on the Philosophy of Life* (New York: MacMillan, 2006); "William James," Wikipedia, https://en.wikipedia.org/wiki/William_James; and "William James: Philosopher, Doctor, Journalist, Psychologist (1842–1910)," Biography, https://www.biography.com/people/william-james-9352726. Works by and on William James are available online at Project Gutenberg, the Internet Archive, and LibriVox.

137. Wilshire, *Primal Roots*, chaps. 3, 4, 5.

138. See Robert D. Richardson, *William James: In the Maelstrom of American Modernism* (New York: Houghton Mifflin, 2006).

139. James, *Writings*, 348, quoted in McKenna and Pratt, *American Philosophy*, 56.

140. Ibid., 644, quoted in McKenna and Pratt, *American Philosophy*, 58.

141. On Charles Sanders Peirce, see McKenna and Pratt, *American Philosophy*, 2, 3, 29, 55–56, 70–73, 90, 93, 170–73, 180, 188, 199, 203, 207–9, 220, 223, 263, 275–76, 293, 306, 330–40, 342–44, 346, 358–61, 370–72, 375–79, 384, 389, 395, 401–4, and chap. 8; Pratt, *Native Pragmatism*, xii, 6–7, 9–10, 20–23, 26, 28, 30, 32–34, 283; Wilshire, *Primal Roots*, ix–x, 5, 12, 17, 42n6, 84, 127, 138, 151n7, 179, 180–81, 187, 204, and chap. 13; *Joseph Brent, Charles Sanders Peirce: A Life, 2nd ed. (Bloomington: Indiana University Press, 1998);* Edward C. Moore and Richard S. Robin, eds., *Studies in the Philosophy of Charles Sanders Peirce* (Amherst: University of Massachusetts Press, 1964); Max Fisch, Kenneth Laine Ketner, and Christian J. W. Kloesel, eds., *Peirce, Semeiotic, and Pragmatism* (Bloomington: Indiana University Press, 1986); Michael L. Raposa, *Peirce's Philosophy of Religion* (Bloomington: Indiana University Press, 1989); Nathan Houser and Christian Kloesel, eds., *Selected Philosophical Writings (1867–1893)*, vol. 1 of *The Essential Peirce* (Bloomington: Indiana University Press, 2009); Peirce Edition Project, ed., *Selected Philosophical Writings (1893–1913)*, vol. 2 of *The Essential Peirce* (Bloomington: Indiana University Press, 2009);

"Charles Sanders Peirce," Wikipedia, https://en.wikipedia.org/wiki/Charles_S._Peirce; and "Charles S. Peirce," Peirce.org, www.peirce.org/. Peirce's collected paper on pragmatism and pragmaticism are available at "Charles Sanders Peirce: The Collected Papers Vol. V: Pragmatism and Pramaticism," Historische Texte & Worterbucher, www.textlog.de/peirce_pragmatism.html. Other writings by Peirce and information about him are also available from Arisbe: The Peirce Gateway, www.iupui.edu/~arisbe/; Digital Encyclopedia of Charles S. Peirce, www.digitalpeirce.fee.unicamp.br/; and Peirce Editions Project (PEP), www.iupui.edu/~peirce/.

142. See the discussion of Peirce's approach to evolution, including its social aspects, in McKenna and Pratt, *American Philosophy*, 64–66.

143. Houser and Christian Kloesel, eds., *The Essential Peirce*, vol. 1, p. 354, quoted in McKenna and Pratt, *American Philosophy*, 64–65.

144. Ibid., 356–57, quoted in McKenna and Pratt, *American Philosophy*, 65.

145. Ibid., quoted in McKenna and Pratt, *American Philosophy*, 65.

146. Ibid., 278, quoted in McKenna and Pratt, *American Philosophy*, 66.

147. On John Dewey, see *Native Pragmatism*, xii, xiv, 7, 9–12, 14, 17–18, 21–22, 25–28, 30–31, 35–38, 56, 72–73, 282, 285–86; McKenna and Pratt, *American Philosophy*, 2, 4–5, 49, 53, 56, 91, 94–95, 105, 122, 149–50, 150–59, 164–67, 170, 173, 180, 188–93, 234, 258–59, 263, 287, 306, 315, 320–21, 330–36, 338, 340–46, 351, 355–59, 362, 371, 375–77, 381–85, 389–90, 399–405, and chap. 11; Wilshire, *Primal Roots*, ix, 3, 7–9, 13, 63, 69, 81, 111, 144, 150, 181, 187–88, 183, 192, 199, 209, 224, and chaps. 6–7; John J. McDermott, ed., *The Philosophy of John Dewey* (Chicago: University of Chicago Press, 1981); Larry Hickman and Thomas Alexander, eds., *The Essential Dewey*, 2 vols. (Bloomington: Indiana University Press, 1998); John Dewey, *The Early Works: 1892–1898*, ed. Jo Ann Boydston (Carbondale: Southern Illinois University Press, 1969–1972); *The Middle Works: 1899–1924, The Later Works: 1925–1953*, and *Supplementary Volume 1: 1884–1951*, ed. Jo Ann Boydston and Larry A. Hickman (Charlottesville, VA: InteLex, 1996); William R. Caspary, *Dewey on Democracy* (Ithaca, NY: Cornell University Press, 2000); Jay Martin, *The Education of John Dewey* (New York: Columbia University Press, 2003); Stephen Rockefeller, *John Dewey: Religious Faith and Democratic Humanism* (New York: Columbia University Press, 1994); A. G. Rud, Jim Garrison, and Lynda Stone, eds., *John Dewey at 150: Reflections for a New Century* (West Lafayette, IN: Purdue University Press, 2009); Alan Ryan, *John Dewey and the High Tide of American Liberalism* (New York: W.

W. Norton, 1995); Robert B. Westbrook, *John Dewey and American Democracy* (Ithaca, NY: Cornell University Press, 1993); Richard J. Bernstein, *John Dewey* (New York: Washington Square, 1966); Raymond Boisvert, *John Dewey: Rethinking Our Time* (Albany: State University of New York Press, 1997); James Campbell, *Understanding John Dewey: Nature and Cooperative Intelligence* (Chicago: Open Court, 1995); "John Dewey," Wikipedia, https://en.wikipedia.org/wiki/John_Dewey; and "John Dewey, American Pragmatist," Pragmatism Cybrary, http://dewey.pragmatism.org/. Works by, and in some case about, John Dewey are available online at Project Gutenberg, the Internet Archive, and LibriVox.

148. Dewey, *The Middle Works*, vol. 12, p. 273, quoted in McKenna and Pratt, *American Philosophy*, 91.

149. Ibid., vol. 10, p. 288, quoted in McKenna and Pratt, *American Philosophy*, 91.

150. Ibid., vol. 14, p. 9, quoted in McKenna and Pratt, *American Philosophy*, 92.

151. John Dewey, *Human Nature and Conduct* [1922] (New York: Modern Library, 1930), 14–15, quoted by Wilshire, *Primal Roots*, 127. See Wilshire's discussion of Dewey's psychology in *Primal Roots*, chap. 7, for more development of what is discussed here on Dewey's psychology.

152. John Dewey, *Experience and Nature* [1922] (New York: Dover, 1958), 316–17, also available in *The Later Works*, vol. 1, 239, quoted by Wilshire, *Primal Roots*, 123.

153. On the known chain of connection between American Indian ways and John Dewey's thought, see Pratt, *Native Pragmatism*, xvi–xvii, 56n1, 214, 215, 268.

154. John Dewey, ed., *John Dewey Presents the Living Thought of Thomas Jefferson* (London: Longman's Green, 1940), also in *The Later Works*, 173–88, 201–23.

155. Pratt, *Native Pragmatism*, xvi–xvii.

156. McKenna and Pratt, *American Philosophy*, chap. 19, 20.

157. Ibid., chap. 16.

158. Ibid., chap. 24.

159. Ibid., chap. 22.

160. On Rorty, in particular, and this issue generally, see ibid., chap. 30.

161. On the post–World War II expansion of American Indian writers having an important impact in the United States, including in the field

of philosophy, see ibid., chap. 30. On the launching of the American Indian Philosophy Association, one of whose meetings was attended by author Stephen Sachs, some information is available in V. F. Cordova, ed., "Newsletter on American Indians in Philosophy," *APA Newsletter* 1, no. 2 (2001), http://c.ymcdn.com/sites/www.apaonline.org/resource/collection/13B1F8E6-0142-45FD-A626-9C4271DC6F62/v01n2AmericanIndians.pdf; and Anne Waters, ed., "Newsletter on American Indians in Philosophy," *APA Newsletter* 2, no. 2 (2003), http://c.ymcdn.com/sites/www.apaonline.org/resource/collection/13B1F8E6-0142-45FD-A626-9C4271DC6F62/v02n2AmericanIndians.pdf. An example of the collaborative writing facilitated by the American Indian Philosophy Association is Anne Waters, ed., *American Indian Thought* (Malden, MA: Blackwell, 2004).

162. The philosophical developments are discussed in McKenna and Pratt, *American Philosophy*, chap. 32. The increasing polarization is discussed below in the introduction to part II, and in chap. 5.

163. Richard Bernstein, *Abuse of Evil: The Corruption of Politics and Religion since 9/11* (Cambridge, UK: Polity, 2005; New York: John Wiley, 2006).

164. Ibid., 120–21.

165. On Obama and pragmatism, see McKenna and Pratt, *American Philosophy*, 370–72.

166. Barack Obama, "Remarks by the President on the Supreme Court Decision on Marriage Equality," White House, Office of the Press Secretary, June 26, 2015, https://obamawhitehouse.archives.gov/the-press-office/2015/06/26/remarks-president-supreme-court-decision-marriage-equality. On the question of President Obama growing on the issue of gay marriage, Zeke J. Miller, "Obama Says He Didn't Mislead on Gay Marriage," *Time*, February 11, 2015, http://time.com/3704760/barack-obama-gay-marriage-david-axelrod/, which reports that: "President Barack Obama maintained in a new interview that he 'evolved' on gay marriage":

Where my evolution took place was not in my attitude toward same-sex couples, it was in understanding the pain and the sense of stigma that was being placed on same-sex couples who are friends of mine, where they'd say, "You know what, if you're not calling it marriage, it doesn't feel like the same thing," Obama told *BuzzFeed*.

Asked specifically about the old questionnaire, Obama offered no explanation for why he said he supported the unions before deciding to oppose them.

"The old questionnaire, you know, is an example of struggling with what was a real issue at the time," Obama said.

167. James T. Kloppenberg, *Reading Obama: Dreams, Hope, and the American Political Tradition* (Princeton, NJ: Princeton University Press, 2011), 92–93 and chap. 1, on his early years, education, and much of his community organizing.

168. B.J.Reyes, "PunahouLeftLastingImpressiononObama," *HonoluluStar-Bulletin,*February10,2007,http://archives.starbulletin.com/2007/02/08/news/story02.html.

169. Matilda Joslyn Gage, *Woman, Church, and State* [1893] (Aberdeen, SD: Sky Carrier, 1998), 15.

170. I received my doctorate from the University of California, Santa Cruz (history of consciousness, concentration on women's studies) in 1978. My dissertation was a preliminary biography of Gage. A founder of the women's studies program at California State University at Sacramento (then Sacramento State College), I taught my first women's studies class in 1970. The program was the third established in the country, with the first minor in women's studies.

171. Paula Gunn Allen, *The Sacred Hoop: Recovering the Feminine in American Indian Traditions* (Boston: Beacon Press, 1986), 213–14.

172. Frederick Douglass, *My Escape from Slavery and Reconstruction,* Project Gutenberg, https://www.gutenberg.org/files/99/99-h/99-h.htm#escape.

173. I first heard this term used by my colleague, Bob Spiegelman, whose website www.sullivanclinton.com/ describes the Sullivan-Clinton Campaign of 1779 as the "largest expedition ever before mounted against the Indians of North America," which he documents with materials "hidden in plain sight."

174. "Declaration of Sentiments: 1848 Women's Rights Convention," Women's History Guide, http://womenshistory.info/declaration-sentiments-1848-womens-rights-convention/.

175. Matilda Joslyn Gage, "The Remnant of the Five Nations," *New York Evening Post*, September 24, 1875.

176. Gage, *Woman, Church, and State,* 6.

177. While references to it appear in her personal papers, the manuscript has been lost.

178. Alice Fletcher, "The Legal Conditions of Indian Women," *Report of the International Council of Women, Assembled by the National Woman Suffrage Association* (Washington, DC: Rufus H. Darby, 1888), 237–41.

179. Ibid.

180. Matilda Joslyn Gage (Alcor), "Green Corn Dance of the Onondagas," *New York Evening Mail*, November 3, 1875.

181. Ibid.

182. Matilda Joslyn Gage, "The Onondaga Indians," *New York Evening Post*, November 3, 1875.

183. This is a seldom used self-name that is still used today by the Haudenosaunee. That Gage knew it indicates a more-than-surface-level knowledge of the culture.

184. Gage, "The Remnant of the Five Nations."

185. Gage, *Woman, Church, and State*, 17–18.

186. While wigwams were used by their woodland Algonquian neighbors, the Haudenosaunee built longhouses, similarly constructed with pole frames and elm bark covering, but much larger than wigwams. Haudenosaunee men did construct the simpler wigwams sometimes when hunting.

187. Gage, *Woman, Church, and State*, 18.

188. My italics. Judith K. Brown, "Iroquois Women: An Ethnohistoric Note," *Toward an Anthropology of Women*, ed. Rayva Reiter (New York: Monthly Review, 1975), 250–51.

189. Matilda Joslyn Gage, "The Mother of His Children," *San Francisco Pioneer*, November 9, 1871.

190. Ibid.

191. Revised Statutes, New York State, Section 1, Title 3, chapter 8, part 2.

192. Gage, "The Mother of His Children."

193. Gage, *Woman, Church, and State*, 18.

194. Sir William Blackstone, *Commentaries on the Laws of England* (Oxford: Clarendon, 1765), 444, 445, and bk. 1, chap. 15.

195. *State vs. Hussey*, 44 N.C. 123, 1852 N.C. Lexis 163, Gilmer 123 (December 1852).

196. *State vs. Jesse Black*, 60 N.C. 266, 1864 N.C. Lexis 23; 1 Win. 266 (June 1864).

197. *State v. A. B. Rhodes*, 61 N.C. 453, 1868 N.C. Lexis 38, 1 Phil. Law 453 (January 1868).

198. Elizabeth Cady Stanton, Susan B. Anthony, and Matilda Joslyn Gage, eds., *History of Woman Suffrage*, vol. 1 (Rochester, NY: Susan B. Anthony, 1881), 88–89.

199. Elizabeth Cady Stanton, "The Matriarchate," *The National Bulletin* 1 (February 1891), 5.

200. Elizabeth Cady Stanton, "On Marriage and Divorce" [1871], Gifts of Speech, http://gos.sbc.edu/s/stantoncady3.html.

201. Fletcher, "The Legal Conditions of Indian Women," 238–39.

202. "Mary Elizabeth Beauchamp Letter," *Skaneateles Democrat*, April 10, 1883. Gage is likely to have had this information. Beauchamp's daughter-in-law wrote a song, "The Battle Hymn of the Suffragists," dedicated to Matilda Joslyn Gage. Gage also wrote short stories for the *Skaneateles Democrat*, edited by Beauchamp's father, in the 1850s.

203. Harriet Maxwell Converse, "New York's Indians," *New York Herald*, February 2, n.d., in *Writings of H. M. Converse and Miscellaneous Scrapbook of Ely S. Parker* (Albany: New York State Museum), 105.

204. Lois W. Banner, *Elizabeth Cady Stanton: A Radical for Woman's Rights* (New York: Little, Brown, 1980), 145.

205. Stanton, "The Matriarchate."

206. Gage, "The Remnant of the Five Nations."

207. Matilda Joslyn (Alcor) Gage, Letter to Helen Leslie Gage, December 11, 1893, Gage Collection, Schlesinger Library, Radcliffe College.

208. Gary Snyder, "Tribalism: Back to the Basics," *Rat: Subterranean News* 2, no. 17 (August 27–September 9, 1969), 3, 8.

209. Ken Kesey, *One Flew over the Cuckoo's Nest* (New York: New American Library, 1963).

210. The book was transformed into a play, *One Flew over the Cuckoo's Nest*, by Dale Wasserman in 1963. Bo Goldman adapted the novel into a 1975 film directed by Miloš Forman, which won five Academy Awards, "One Flew Over the Cuckoo's Nest (novel)," Wikipedia, https://en.wikipedia.org/wiki/One_Flew_Over_the_Cuckoo%27s_Nest_(novel).

211. Sherry L. Smith, *Hippies, Indians, and the Fight for Red Power* (New York: Oxford University Press, 2012), 20.

212. Ibid., 45–51.

213. Ibid., 52.

214. Stewart Brand, *Whole Earth Catalog* (1968), http://wholeearth.com/index.php.

215. Smith, *Hippies, Indians*, 52, 54.

216. Ibid., 56–58.

217. Ibid., 65, 70.

218. Ibid., 59–62.

219. Miriam Hahn, "Playing Hippies and Indians: Acts of Cultural Colonization in the Theatre of the American Counterculture" (PhD diss., Bowling Green State University, 2014), citing Timothy Hodgdon, *Manhood in the Age of Aquarius: Masculinity in Two Countercultural Communities, 1965–83* (New York: Columbia University Press, 2007).

220. Hahn, "Playing Hippies and Indians," 81–82, citing Hodgdon, *Manhood in the Age of Aquarius,* xxvii; and Dominick Cavallo, *A Fiction of the Past: The Sixties in American History* (New York: St. Martin's, 1999), 12.

221. Hahn, "Playing Hippies and Indians," 81, citing Bradford D. Martin, *The Theatre Is in the Street: Politics and Public Performance in Sixties America* (Amherst: University of Massachusetts Press, 2004), 87.

222. Peter Coyote, *Sleeping Where I Fall* (Washington, DC: Counterpoint, 1998).

223. Cited in Hahn, "Playing Hippies and Indians," 82.

224. Ibid., 87, citing an interview.

225. Smith, *Hippies, Indians,* 119–20.

226. Timothy Miller, *The 60s Communes: Hippies and Beyond* (Syracuse, NY: Syracuse University Press, 1999), 155.

227. Lewis Yablonsky, *The Hippie Trip* (New York: Pegasus, 1968), 301.

228. Miller, *The 60s Communes,* 153.

229. Ibid.

230. Ibid., 201.

231. William Hedgepeth, *The Alternative: Communal Life in New America* (New York: Macmillan, 1970), 187.

232. Smith, *Hippies, Indians,* 126–27, 143.

233. Black Elk, *Black Elk Speaks: Being the Life Story of a Holy Man of the Oglala Sioux* [1932], ed. John G. Neihardt (New York: Pocket, 1959).

234. Wallace Black Elk and William S. Lyon, *Black Elk: The Sacred Ways of a Lakota* (New York: Harper and Row, 1990). Also, author Stephen Sachs's direct interactions with Wallace Black Elk and Indian people who worked with him in the 1980s and 1990s.

235. Earth Circle Association Newsletters of the 1990s, published in Yreka, California, and author Stephen Sachs's discussions with Earth Circle people.

236. Direct experience of author Stephen Sachs and discussions he had with Bertha Grove, her family members, and non-Indians who worked with them, beginning in 1987. Sachs has supported the Southern Ute

Sun Dance regularly since 1986, and more recently has been participating in the tribe's Bear Dance, and has maintained a close association with the Grove-Birch-Naranjo Family, as well as with others at
the Southern Ute Reservation.

237. This was said by Sufi leader Abdul Aziz Said at the Omega Institute
in the early 1980s, with author Stephen Sachs present.

238. Doug Boyd, *Rolling Thunder* (New York: Dell, 1974). A brief biography
of John Pope is provided in "Rolling Thunder (person)," Wikipedia,
https://en.wikipedia.org/wiki/Rolling_Thunder_(person).

239. "The True Story of 'The Crying Indian,'" Priceonomics, https://pri-
ceonomics.com/the-true-story-of-the-crying-indian/.

240. Miller, *The 60s Communes*, 223.

241. Timothy Miller, *The Hippies and American Values*, 2nd ed. (Knoxville:
University of Tennessee Press, 2011), 7–8, cited in Hahn, "Playing
Hippies and Indians," 133–34.

242. Hahn, "Playing Hippies and Indians," 133.

243. Smith, *Hippies, Indians*, 142, citing Philip J. Deloria, *Playing Indian*
(New Haven, CT: Yale University Press, 1998).

244. Smith, *Hippies, Indians*, 143.

245. The connection between the counterculture and more effective
Indian political action has been explored in such works as George
Pierre Castile, *To Show Heart: Native American Self-Determination and
Federal Indian Policy, 1960–1990* (Tucson: University of Arizona Press,
1998); George Pierre Castile, *Taking Charge: Native American Self-
Determination and Federal Indian Policy, 1975–1993* (Tucson: University
of Arizona Press, 2006); Paul Chaat Smith and Robert Allen Warrior,
*Like a Hurricane: The American Indian Movement from Alcatraz to Wounded
Knee* (New York: New Press, 1996); Charles Wilkinson, *Blood Struggle:
The Rise of Modern Indian Nations*, pt. 2 (New York: W. W. Norton, 2005);
James S. Olson and Raymond Wilson, *Native Americans in the Twentieth
Century* (Urbana: University of Illinois Press, 1984), chaps. 7–8.

246. Smith, *Hippies, Indians*, 144.

247. Ibid., 156–57, 171, 217.

248. Castile, *To Show Heart*; Smith and Warrior, *Like a Hurricane*; Wilkinson,
Blood Struggle, pt. 2; Olson and Wilson, *Native Americans in the Twentieth
Century*, chaps. 7–8.

249. Castile, *To Show Heart*; Smith and Warrior, *Like a Hurricane*;
Wilkinson, *Blood Struggle*, pt. 2; Olson and Wilson, *Native Americans
in the Twentieth Century*, chaps. 7–8; and Harris, Sachs, and Morris,
Re-Creating the Circle, chap. 3, sec. 1).

250. Jane L. Levere, "After the 'Crying Indian,' Keep America Beautiful Starts a New Campaign," *New York Times,* July 16, 2013, www.nytimes. com/2013/07/17/business/media/decades-after-a-memorable-campaign-keep-america-beautiful-returns.html. A version of this article appeared in print on July 17, 2013, on page B5 of the New York edition and reported: "On Earth Day in 1971, the two organizations [Keep America Beautiful and the Ad Council] introduced the 'crying Indian' commercial, which was created by Marsteller Advertising and featured the actor Iron Eyes Cody paddling a canoe through polluted waters and crying at the spectacle. Ad Age named the advertising—which was aimed at promoting individual responsibility in protecting the environment and ran until 1983—one of the top 100 campaigns of the 20th century."

251. Mike Gabriel and Eric Goldberg, dirs., *Pocahontas,* produced by Walt Disney Feature Animation and released by Walt Disney Pictures. See Roger Ebert, "Pocahontas," [review] RogerEbert.com, June 16, 1995, www.rogerebert.com/reviews/pocahontas-1995. The film emphasizes the ecological aspect of a changing view of Indians in a changing US culture, with many subplots and many interweaving and to different degrees interacting strands, as partly developed in the introduction to part II of this book. On the development of stereotypes of American Indians, see Brian W. Dippie, "American Indians: The Image of the Indian," TeacherServe, http://nationalhumanitiescenter.org/tserve/nattrans/ntecoindian/essays/indimage.htm; Robert F. Berkhofer Jr., *The White Man's Indian: Images of the American Indian from Columbus to the Present* (New York: Alfred A. Knopf, 1978).

252. Anna J. Willow, "Images of American Indians in Environmental Education: Anthropological Reflections on the Politics and History of Cultural Representation," *American Indian Culture and Research Journal* 34, no. 1 (2010): 67–88:

For hundreds of years, North America's colonizers worked systematically to eradicate the indigenous cultural practices, religious beliefs, and autonomous political systems many venerate. This article illustrates that imperialist nostalgia underlies and directs portrayals of American Indians in environmental education today. Whether unconsciously or unmistakably, intellectual insight is often born of personal experience. This article presents the author's critical perspective on the politics and history of American Indian cultural representation which took shape in the place where academic and applied fields collide, where work weaves itself into the fabric of everyday life. The author argues that environmental education's enduring fascination with Native Americans can be understood as a symptomatic manifestation of non-Native society's collective imperialist nostalgia for the purportedly environmentally sustainable indigenous ways of life it destroyed. Portrayals of American Indians in environmental education are built upon the simultaneous erasure of contemporary Native realities and the glorification of a selectively monolithic Native past; they combine a denial of actual Indian peoples' coevalness with calls for inventive emulation by non-Indians.

253. That Thoreau is foundational to the environmental movement—and also Ralph Waldo Emerson—is discussed in section 2, above, and by Erin McKenna and Scott Pratt, *American Philosophy: From Wounded Knee to the Present* (New York: Bloomsbury, 2016), chap. 21, among other things, noting that John Muir (1838–1914) and Emerson were exchanging ideas with each other, and Aldo Leopold (1887–1948) also was greatly impacted by Thoreau and Emerson concerning human relations with nature, and that the Thoreauian stream of thought was continued by environmentalists in the 1950s and later.

254. Henry David Thoreau, *The Journal of Henry D. Thoreau* (Boston: Houghton Mifflin, 1906); Bradley P. Dean, "Thoreau's Indians: A Compilation of Indian References," a listing with quotations from the journals that Dean sent to Connie Baxter Marlow via email in 2005 found more than 1,900 references to Indians in Thoreau's journals. She in turn shared the compilation with the authors of this book.

255. Henry David Thoreau, "Life without Principle," in *Thoreau: Collected Essays and Poems* (New York: Library of America, 2001), para. 15.

256. Ibid.

257. R. F. Sayre, *Thoreau and the American Indians* (Princeton, NJ: Princeton University Press, 1977), 8.

258. Ibid., 19.

259. Thoreau, *Journal*, May 9, 1841, 4101–6.

260. Thoreau, *Journal*, August 18, 1841, 4107–12.

261. Thoreau, *Journal* (Long Book Fall 1842–1844), PEJ2-00'-060.

262. "Starts a New Campaign."

263. Henry Smith, "Chief Seattle's 1854 Oration," *Seattle Sunday Star,* October 29, 1887, para. 5, www.halcyon.com/arborhts/chiefsea. html.

264. Ibid., para. 4.

265. The reading of the Bible as saying that human beings have "dominion" over the earth has often been contested. Pope Francis, in his environmental encyclical, for example, states that this reading is a misunderstanding. He states that the true reading of the passage calls for "stewardship," not "dominion." But even if one reads the passage to say "dominion," or "rule over," that may not mean that human beings have the right to do anything they wish with nature. The long tradition of rulership in the West going back, at least, to Plato in the *Republic,* Book II (in the discussion with Thrasimicus), Aristotle in the *Politics* and *Nicomachean Ethics,* and Saint Thomas Aquinas in the *Suma Theologica,* is that rulership is for the good of the ruled, and hence a form of stewardship. It is only if one assumes, as Locke does under a social contract, in *The Second Treatise on Government,* that the gifts of nature are essentially unlimited when properly developed, that the "dominion" interpretation becomes extremely environmentally destructive.

266. Smith, "Chief Seattle's 1854 Oration," para. 10.

267. On the Polynesians and others see J. Baird Callicott, *Earth's Insights: A Survey of Ecological Ethics from the Mediterranean Basin to the Australian Outback* (Berkeley: University of California Press, 1994).

268. Black Elk, *Black Elk Speaks,* 164–65.

269. Barry Commoner, *The Closing Circle* (New York: Alfred A. Knopf, 1971), 298–99.

270. Lynn White, "The Historical Roots of Our Ecologic Crisis," *Science* 155 (March 10, 1967), also appears in David Spring and Eileen Spring, eds., *Ecology and Religion in History* (New York: Harper and Row, 1974), introduction.

271. Genesis 1:26. But note, this is the common modern Western translation of the Hebrew, and others are possible. This includes those that are more eco-centered, and read the passage as requiring humans to have a responsibility to be stewards of the environment, as Pope Francis sets forth in his environmental encyclical, discussed below. Some critics of the destructive "dominion" interpretation of Genesis point out that God created the land and the sea, and the creatures thereof, before creating human beings (Genesis 1:24–26 and 2:7,19),

and told Adam to give the creatures names. As coauthor of *Honoring the Circle*, Donna K. Dial points out, it is difficult to understand that having given Adam the authority to name nonhuman beings, s/he would give permission to destroy them.

272. Ibid., 1:28

273. White, "The Historical Roots of Our Ecologic Crisis."

274. Ibid., p. 5.

275. T. C. McLuhan, *Touch the Earth: A Self-Portrait of Indian Existence* (New York: Touchstone, 1971), 45.

276. Rousseau's writing is open to various interpretations. Some would see his view of Indians as more solitary, others as closer to their own worldview, as communal, but with the individuality that follows the principle of place, or diversity, within the circle of relationships.

277. See Gregory Cajete, *Native Science: Natural Laws of Interdependence* (Santa Fe, NM: Clear Light, 2000), on the advanced development of Indigenous agriculture in the Americas and on other aspects of Native equivalents of "science."

278. McLuhan, *Touch the Earth*.

279. David Barnhill, "Deep Ecology," Encyclopedia of Earth, October 12, 2006 (updated April 30, 2012), www.eoearth.org/view/article/151670/.

280. Bron Taylor, *Dark Green Religion: Nature Spirituality and the Planetary Future* (Berkeley: University of California Press, 2013); and Bron Taylor, ed., *The Encyclopedia of Religion and Nature* (London: Continuum International, 2005). Taylor has served as president of the International Society for the Study of Religion, Nature, and Culture, and editor of the *Journal for the Study of Religion, Nature, and Culture*.

281. Aldo Leopold, *A Sand County Almanac* (New York: Oxford University Press, 1949), 204.

282. Ibid., 204.

283. Ibid., 210. Moreover, the shallower view of "conservation," which separates human beings from nature, and has an essentially capitalist economic aspect, often leads to exploitation or degradation of human beings, and may be counterproductive to its conservation goals. For example, a number of conservation organizations, including the World Wildlife Fund, and a number of governments have been involved in removing Indigenous people from their homes in nature preserves, against their will, usually destroying their way of life, and often without compensation. Usually there is an economic

incentive of increasing tourism as part of the reason for establishing the nature reserve. This removal is a serious violation of human rights and the International Declaration of the Rights of Indigenous Peoples. In addition, it fails to recognize that Indigenous peoples are usually the best stewards of the environment. This was shown in "Revealed: Tiger Numbers Increase When Tribes Stay in Tiger Reserves," Survival International, December 9, 2015, www.survivalinternational.org/news/11004, which reported:

Startling new data reveals tiger numbers have increased rapidly in the first reserve in India where local tribes have won the right to stay. The information, which the Indian National Tiger Conservation Authority originally tried to suppress, discredits government policy to remove the many tribes whose lands have been turned into tiger reserves.

Between 2010 and 2014 the tiger population in the BRT Tiger Reserve in Karnataka state almost doubled, from 35 to 68. Unlike elsewhere in India, local Soliga people have been allowed to continue living alongside tigers, even in the core of the reserve. This increase is far higher than the national rate at which the tiger population is growing.

The Soliga have a highly developed relationship with their natural environment, and venerate the tiger. Madegowda, a Soliga man, said, "We worship tigers as gods. There hasn't been a single incident of conflict with tigers and Soligas or hunting here."

Across India, tribal communities are being broken up and evicted from their ancestral lands in the name of tiger conservation. In 2014, hundreds of Baiga tribespeople were evicted from Kanha Tiger Reserve—home of Rudyard Kipling's "Jungle Book"—while over a hundred thousand tourists are welcomed into the reserve every year.

Survival International, the global movement for tribal people's rights, is calling for a new conservation model that respects tribal peoples' rights and uses their expertise to protect and enhance ecological diversity. Tribal peoples are better at looking after their environment than anyone else: they are the best conservationists and guardians of the natural world.

Survival's Director Stephen Corry said, "These figures expose government policy to remove tribespeople from tiger reserves as not only immoral but also counterproductive. Tigers tend to do well when tribal communities remain—they have, after all, lived together for generations. But unlike tribal people, the thousands of tourists who drive in every day bring in a huge amount of money to the conservation industry. They also, of course, get the tigers used to close human presence—something poachers find useful. The best way to save the tiger is to leave the tribes that have protected their forests alone. Survival will continue to fight and expose the forced evictions that the conservation industry has tried hard to keep hidden."

See also "Tribal Conservationists: No Tribes, No Nature, No Future," Survival International, www.survivalinternational.org/conservation; and "Parks Need Peoples," Survival International, 2014, http://assets.survivalinternational.org/documents/1324/parksneed-peoples-report.pdf, which more fully develops the problem and evidence. Both of these latter articles mention the World Wildlife Fund as supporting actions to remove Indigenous peoples from preserves.

More recent evidence that Indigenous people are the best protectors of the environment where they live comes from Guatemala, where for fifteen years, as of 2015, in sections of the Maya Biosphere Reserve, local Indigenous communities have been policing the forest. In their areas, unlike many other locations, deforestation has been virtually nonexistent (Elisabeth Malkin, "Guatemalans Living Off Forests Get the Task of Saving Them," *New York Times*, November 26, 2015).

284. J. Baird Callicott, *In Defense of the Land Ethic* (Albany: State University of New York Press, 1989), 197. Callicott has been an initiator of the field of environmental ethics. As of 2015, he was a University Distinguished Research Professor and a member of the Department of Philosophy and Religion Studies and the Institute of Applied Sciences at the University of North Texas, having previously served as professor of philosophy and natural resources at the University of Wisconsin–Stevens Point from 1969 to 1995, where he taught the world's first

course in environmental ethics in 1971. From 1994 to 2000, he served as vice president then president of the International Society for Environmental Ethics. Callicott has authored numerous publications on environmental ethics and related issues, many of which are listed in "J. Baird Callicott," Wikipedia, https://en.wikipedia.org/wiki/J._Baird_Callicott. See also Ann Causey, "Callicott, John Baird," in *Environmental Encyclopedia*, ed. W. P. Cunningham et al. (Detroit, MI: Gale Research, 1994), 124; Michael Egan, "Callicott, J. Baird," in *American Environmental Leaders: From Colonial Times to the Present*, ed. Ann Becher, Kyle McClure, Rachel White Scheuering, and Julia Willis, vol. 1 (Santa Barbara, CA: ABC CLIO, 2001), 141–43; Y. S. Lo, "Callicott, J. Baird 1941–," in *Encyclopedia of Environmental Ethics and Philosophy*, ed. J. Baird Callicott and Robert Frodeman (New York: Macmillan Reference, 2008), 129–30; Michael P. Nelson, "J. Baird Callicott, 1941–," in *Fifty Key Thinkers on the Environment*, ed. Joy A. Palmer (London: Routledge, 2001), 290–95; Michael P. Nelson, "Callicott, J. Baird (1941–)," in *Encyclopedia of Religion and Nature*, ed. Bron Taylor and Jeffrey Kaplan (London: Continuum International, 2005), 252–54; Clare Palmer and Bron Taylor, eds., "Special Theme Issue on J. Baird Callicott's Earth's Insights," *Worldviews: Environment, Culture, Religion* 1, no. 2 (1997); and Wayne Ouderkirk and Jim Hill, eds., *Land, Value, and Community: Callicott and Environmental Philosophy* (Albany: State University of New York Press, 2002). The large number of references to Callicott in works on the environment, including encyclopedias, is testimony to his importance in the development of the movement.

285. On the impact of American Indians in Europe, see chapter 3 of this book. As the authors have not inquired into the sources of Hume's thinking, it is not possible to know if at all, and if so, to what extent, his views may have been partially inspired, or reinforced, either directly or indirectly (including by Rousseau) by Indigenous Americans. What is clear is that American Indian ideas and ways of seeing were widely discussed in some of the circles he was involved with, including his time with Jesuits in France, whose order sent back a huge number of reports from "New France" (Canada) on Indians, as is discussed in chapter 3. See Thomas Henry Huxley, *Hume* (Cambridge: Cambridge University Press, 2011), 7–8.

286. This is only one view. From another viewpoint, what can be shown empirically is factual. And if one can assert or agree that what harms people is bad and should be avoided, then if it can be shown

empirically that global warming is caused by human action and that global warming harms people, then that action is bad, and action should be taken to avoid global warming. To take this view about fact and logic does not, in itself, denigrate feeling or emotion. How important they are is a separate question. For Callicott, most deep ecologists, and the authors of this section of the book, who take a holistic view, feeling is definitely important.

287. Leopold, *Sand County Almanac*, 223.

288. Ibid., 223–23.

289. The ongoing process of Native American renewal after physical and cultural genocide is considered holistically in Harris, Sachs, and Morris, *Re-Creating the Circle*. Chapter 2 gives an overview of the genocide and the continuing problems it has caused, while many sources for more detailed accounts are provided.

290. On Gray Owl (Archibald Belaney), see John Sugden, "From the Land of Shadows: The Making of Grey Owl," [review] *American Indian Quarterly* 15, no. 3 (1991); Grey Owl, *Pilgrims of the Wild* (Toronto, ON: Dundurn, 2010); Donald B. Smith, *From the Land of Shadows: The Making of Grey Owl* (Saskatoon, SK: Western Prairie, 1990); Tina Loo, *States of Nature: Conserving Canada's Wildlife in the Twentieth Century* (Vancouver: UBC Press, 2006); and "Grey Owl," Wikipedia, https://en.wikipedia.org/wiki/Grey_Owl.

291. Thomas E. Mails and Dan Evehema, *Hotevilla: Hopi Shrine of the Covenant; Microcosm of the World* (New York: Marlowe, 1995). Evehema was one of the four Hopis selected by his Kiva to take the Hopi prophesies to the wider world. Mails and Evehema, *Hotevilla*, and Thomas E. Mails, *The Hopi Survival Kit* (New York: Stewart, Tabori, and Chang, 1997), discuss the Hopi prophecies; a consideration of the gourd of ashes, the house of mica, and the Hopi journeys are discussed in the latter (95–96), and some of the environmental concerns are discussed in chap. 10. See also Banyacya, Letter to UN Secretary General Perez de Cuellar, October 22, 1991, http://banyacya.indigenousnative.org/preun92.html, concerning his forthcoming fourth visit to the United Nations, and the statement of Banyacya on his mission, with three others, beginning in 1948, in which he says, "Traditional Hopi follow the spiritual path that was given to us by Massau'u the Great Spirit. We made a sacred covenant to follow his life plan…taking care of this land and life. Our goals are not to gain political control or monetary wealth, but to pray and to promote the welfare of all living beings and to preserve the world in a

natural way." Hopi Traditional Elder Thomas Banyacya: Message to the World, http://banyacya.indigenousnative.org (which has links to other sources on Banyacya and Hopi tradition).

292. Banyacya's Letter to Perez de Cuellar, October 22, 1991, mentions working with Oren Lyons, Faith Keeper of his Onondaga clan and others. In 1992, author Stephen Sachs was co-conference chair organizing the annual conference of the Consortium on Peace, Research, Education, and Development (COPRED) with an American Indian focus, "Recreating the Circle: Peace and Justice in the Next 500 Years." On arranging with Oren Lyons that he would participate in the conference, Lyons gave Sachs Banyacya's contact information and suggested that Banyacya be included in the meeting, which he was. Lyons spoke with Sachs at the conference about how Banyacya and a few other Indian leaders traveled together to speak on various issues, including on the environment, about which Lyons was extremely concerned.

293. Some of this geographically broadened Indigenous environmental activity is discussed in Stephen M. Sachs, "Climate Change, Environmental Decay, and Indigenous People: Indigenizing the Greening of the World," *Indigenous Policy* 19, no. 2 (2008).

294. Chief Oren Lyons, "Preamble," John Mohawk, "Introduction," and Jose Barreiro, "Afterword," in *A Basic Call to Consciousness*, ed. Akwesasne Notes (Rooseveltown, NY: Akwesasne Notes, 1978), 71–72. All three are Native and have been extremely active on environmental and a variety of other Indigenous issues.

295. Ibid., 73.

296. See Marija Gimbutas, *The Language of the Goddess: Unearthing the Hidden Symbols of Western Civilization* (San Francisco, CA: Harper, 1989); and Marija Gimbutas, *The Civilization of the Goddess: The World of Old Europe* (San Francisco, CA: Harper, 1991).

297. Akwesasne Notes, ed., *A Basic Call to Consciousness*.

298. Ibid., 76–77.

299. Ibid., 77.

300. On Thomas Aquinas and his work, see "Saint Thomas Aquinas," *Stanford Encyclopedia of Philosophy,* first published July 12, 1999 (substantive revision May 23, 2014), http://plato.stanford.edu/entries/aquinas/#LifeWork; James A. Weisheipl, *Thomas D'Aquino: His Life, Thought, and Work* (Washington, DC: Catholic University of America Press, 1974); and Ralph McInerny, *Thomas Aquinas Selected Writings* (London: Penguin Classics), 1988.

301. In addition to works already cited concerning the Hopi prophecy, see Harold Coulander, *The Fourth World of the Hopis: The Epic Story of the Hopi Indians as Preserved in Their Legends and Traditions* (Albuquerque: University of New Mexico Press, 1987); Frank Waters, *The Book of the Hopi* (New York: Ballentine, 1963); John Hogue, *The Essential Hopi Prophecies* (Honolulu, HI: Hogue, 2015); Dennis Wall and Virgil Masayesva, "People of the Corn: Teachings in Hopi Traditional Agriculture, Spirituality, and Sustainability," *American Indian Quarterly* 28, no. 3–4 (2004): 435–53; Karl Kernberger, prod. and ed., *Hopi Prophecy*, VHS (Princeton, NJ: Films for the Humanities and Sciences, 1994); and Godfrey Reggio, dir., *Koyaanisqatsi* [life out of balance], IRE Productions, Santa Fe Institute for Regional Education, 1982, an art film/avant-garde opera experimental film with music by Philip Glass and cinematography by Ron Fricke.

302. "Ongoing Activities," *Indigenous Policy Journal* 15, no. 3 (2004).

303. Ibid.

304. Mary B. Davis, ed., *Native America in the Twentieth Century: An Encyclopedia* (New York: Garland, 1996), 399; Winona LaDuke, Bruce A. Johansen, and Donald A. Grinde Jr., *An Encyclopedia of Native American Biography* (New York: Henry Holt, 1997), 203; and Winona LaDuke, "Indigenous Environmental Perspectives: A North American Primer," *Akwe:kon Journal* 9, no. 2 (1992): 52–71; Honor the Earth, www.honorearth.org.

305. Honor the Earth.

306. Reported in "Economic Developments," *Indigenous Policy* 16, no. 1 (2005).

307. Michelle Lanteri, "Collateral Damage: Jaun Wuyick-to-See-Smith's Call to Action to Americans to Identify with Environmental Issues," paper presented at Southwest Popular and American Culture Association Conference, Albuquerque, NM, 2015; Jaune Quick-to-See Smith, http://jaunequick-to-seesmith.com.

308. Gail Tremblay, "Jaune Quick-to-See Smith: Flathead Contemporary Artist," Missoula Art Museum, www.missoulaartmuseum.org/files/documents/collection/Montana%20Connections_Smith/TremblayEssay.pdf.

309. On the Morengo, see "Indian and Indigenous Developments: US Developments; Economic Developments," *Indigenous Policy* 14, no. 2 (2003), developed from a statement by Morongo Band of Mission Indians of California tribal chairman Maurice Lyons reported in

an email "Digest of Indigenous News" from Andre Cramblit. On the Navajo solar power development, "Economic Developments," *Indigenous Policy* 16, no. 1 (2005); on Laguna Pueblo designer Dave Melton and Sacred Power Corporation of Albuquerque bringing electricity to isolated homes on the Navajo Reservation, see Sarah Moses, "Seeking Solutions For Global Warming," *Indian Country Today*, December 8, 2006.

310. Sachs, "Climate Change, Environmental Decay, and Indigenous People."

311. Harris, Sachs, and Morris, *Re-Creating the Circle*, chap. 3.

312. David Melmer, "Tribal Colleges Can Play a Role in Fighting Climate Change," *Indian Country Today*, October 17, 2007; and David Melmer, "US Geological Survey, Tribal Colleges Partner for Climate Change Research," *Indian Country Today*, September 17, 2007.

313. "Education and Cultural Developments," *Indigenous Policy* 18, no. 3 (2007).

314. National Congress of American Indians, Accessed December 30, 2018, www.ncai.org.

315. Moses, "Seeking Solutions for Global Warming."

316. National Tribal Environmental Council, www.ntec.org; Institute for Tribal Environmental Professionals, Northern Arizona University, http://www7.nau.edu/itep/main/Home/; National Environmental Coalition of Native Americans, http://necona.indigenousnative. org; Native American Fish and Wildlife Society, www.nafws.org; Native American Water Association, www.nawainc.org; Northwest Indian Fisheries Commission, http://nwifc.org; and Indigenous Environmental Network, www.ienearth.org.

317. "Indigenous Press Conference Demanding True Climate Solutions at COP21," Indigenous Environmental Network, December 3, 2015.

318. Multinational corporate actions creating serious environmental problems for Indigenous peoples are reported regularly in the "Environmental Activities," "Environmental Developments," and "International Indigenous Developments" sections at Indigenous Policy, www.indigenouspolicy.org.

319. On the UN NGO/DPI meeting, see "American Indian and International Indigenous Developments," *Indigenous Policy* 18, no. 3 (2007). Concerning the Indigenous Working Group in the UN Climate Caucus, author Stephen Sachs was the junior co-coordinator, working with Chapter Coordinator-in-Chief Moki Kokoris. The working group sent a report to the secretary-general, "Impacts of

Climate Change on Indigenous Peoples and Their Responses and Effects."

320. Reports of the annual forum meetings are also carried in the "International Developments" section of the spring or summer issues of *Indigenous Policy*, www.indigenouspolicy.org. Also see United Nations: Indigenous Peoples, United Nations Permanent Forum on Indigenous Issues [Facebook page], www.facebook.com/unpfii/.

321. The "Environmental Activities," "International Activities," and "International Developments" sections of *Indigenous Policy* contain reports of international Indigenous activity.

322. "Biography of the Holy Father, Francis," Libreria Editrice Vaticana, http://w2.vatican.va/content/francesco/en/biography/documents/papa-francesco-biografia-bergoglio.html.

323. The entire encyclical, "Encyclical Letter *Laudato Si'* of the Holy Father Francis on Care for Our Common Home" is available at http://w2.vatican.va/content/francesco/en/encyclicals/documents/papa-francesco_20150524_enciclica-laudato-si.html.

324. Lauren McCauley, "Pope Francis Apologizes to Mexican Indigenous for History of Pillage and Abuse," *Common Dreams*, February 16, 2016, www.commondreams.org/news/2016/02/16/pope-francis-apologizes-mexican-indigenous-history-pillage-and-abuse.

325. Except where otherwise noted, the Standing Rock Protest and DAPL developments have been written on the basis of a large number of reports summarized and cited in the "Environmental Activities" and "Environmental Developments" sections of *Indigenous Policy* (Winter and Summer 2017; Winter 2018), plus discussion and communications by Stephen Sachs with people who participated in the Standing Rock DAPL protests. Extended overviews of these events can be found at "Dakota Access Pipeline," Wikipedia, https://en.wikipedia.org/wiki/Dakota_Access_Pipeline; and "Dakota Access Pipeline Protest," Wikipedia, https://en.wikipedia.org/wiki/Dakota_Access_Pipeline_protests#cite_note-army.mil-111.

326. Andrea Germanos, "First Nations Vow: There Will Be No Tar Sands Pipeline," *Common Dreams*, June 12, 2014, www.commondreams.org/headline/2014/06/12-4, reported: "'We have drawn a line in the earth they cannot, and will not, cross,' said Chief Martin Louie of the Nadleh Whut'en First Nation. That is the message stressed by First Nations communities who say that even if Canada's Prime Minister Harper gives the federal OK to Enbridge's Northern Gateway project, First Nations law and their 'responsibilities to future generations'

will stop the project dead in its tracks." In the United States, there were numerous protests against the Keystone XL Pipeline construction going back to 2011. Some of this is discussed in Jane Mayer, "Taking It to the Streets," *The New Yorker*, November 28, 2011. A more comprehensive discussion of the Keystone XL Pipeline is in "Keystone Pipeline," Wikipedia, https://en.wikipedia.org/wiki/Keystone_Pipeline.

327. Amy Goodman, "Video: Dakota Access Pipeline Company Attacks Native American Protesters with Dogs and Pepper Spray," *Democracy Now!*, September 4, 2016, www.democracynow.org/2016/9/4/dakota_access_pipeline_company_attacks_native.

328. Susan Phillips, "Invoking Power of Eminent Domain, Gas Industry Runs Roughshod over Private Property," StateImpact Pennsylvania, May 10, 2016, https://stateimpact.npr.org/pennsylvania/2016/05/10/39687/.

329. "Amnesty International USA to Monitor to North Dakota Pipeline Protests," Amnesty International USA, October 28, 2017, www.amnestyusa.org/press-releases/amnesty-international-usa-to-monitor-to-north-dakota-pipeline-protests/.

330. "Dakota Access Pipeline Protests Spread to 300 Cities as Pipeline Owner Sues to Continue Construction," *Democracy Now!*, November 16, 2016, www.democracynow.org/2016/11/16/nodapl_protests_spread_to_300_cities.

331. Cassi Alexandra and Ariel Zambelich, "Protesters Mark a Solemn Thanksgiving Day at Standing Rock," NPR, November 25, 2016, www.npr.org/sections/thetwo-way/2016/11/25/503278053/protesters-mark-a-solemn-thanksgiving-day-at-standing-rock; Frank Ponciano, "Commentary: San Jose Taking a Stand with Standing Rock Sioux," Mercury News, November 23, 2016, www.mercurynews.com/2016/11/23/ponciano-standing-rock-sioux-need-silicon-valleys-help/; "Northcentral Wisconsin Pipeline Protesters Spend Thanksgiving at Standing Rock," WAOW, November 24, 2017, www.waow.com/story/33790499/northcentral-wisconsin-pipeline-protesters-spend-thanksgiving-at-standing-rock; "To Standing Rock from Rural Oregon: From Our Friends at Rural Organizing Project (ROP)," CALC (Clergy and Laymen Concerned), January 10, 2017, www.calclane.org/to-standing-rock-from-rural-oregon/.

International objections to DAPL included a statement by the International Indigenous Peoples' Forum on Climate Change (IIPFCC) that said, in part, "The International Indigenous Peoples'

Forum on Climate Change (IIPFCC) condemns the construction of the Dakota Access pipeline and stands in solidarity with our sisters and brothers of the Standing Rock Sioux Tribe and all Water Protectors in opposition to this project," as quoted from "The International Indigenous Peoples' Forum on Climate Change Condemns the Construction of the Dakota Access Pipeline," *Cultural Survival*, November 10, 2016, www.culturalsurvival.org/news/international-indigenous-peoples-forum-climate-change-condemns-construction-dakota-access.

332. Author Stephen Sachs, a member of the Sierra Club of Albuquerque, New Mexico, intergroup Energy Committee, was involved in the organizing of two of these actions at Army Corps of Engineers facilities, and participated in them.

333. Forum News Service, "Corps: More Discussion Needed Before Agency Will Approve Dakota Access Easement," *Bemidji Pioneer*, November 14, 2016.

334. US Army, "Army Will Not Grant Easement for Dakota Access Pipeline Crossing" [press release], December 4, 2017; and Amy Dalrymple, "Updated: Corps Denies Easement to Complete Dakota Access Pipeline Construction in N.D.," *Bemidji Pioneer*, December 5, 2016, www.bemidjipioneer.com/news/4172349-updated-corps-denies-easement-complete-dakota-access-pipeline-construction-nd.

335. Steven Mufson, "Trump Gives Green Light to Dakota Access Keystone XL Oil Pipelines," *Washington Post*, January 24, 2017, www.washingtonpost.com/news/energy-environment/wp/2017/01/24/trump-gives-green-light-to-dakota-access-keystone-xl-oil-pipelines/.

336. "Dakota Access Pipeline Is Officially Operational," Indigenous Environmental Network, June 2, 2017, www.mynewsletterbuilder.com/email/newsletter/1413028736. Text of story:

Yesterday, June 1st, Energy Transfer Partners (ETP), the parent company of the Dakota Access Pipeline (DAPL) announced that DAPL is officially fully operational.

This comes just a week after documents were leaked by a TigerSwan contractor revealing that Energy Transfer Partners was involved in using counterterrorist tactics on nonviolent Water Protectors. What's more is that DAPL has already had three oil spills during test runs, this adds to ETP's already bad track record of being responsible for oil spills, yet taking very little account-ability to clean spills up or prevent future spills.

While the pipeline is fully operational a federal judge in the US Court of Appeals still holds the power to halt the project.

Statement from the Indigenous Environmental Network:

We must not lose sight of why the movement against the Dakota Access Pipeline began.

The pipeline was originally set to go through Bismarck, ND but the community rejected that plan because they were afraid it would jeopardize the Bismarck water supply. Thereafter the pipeline was routed to pass thru treaty lands of the Oceti Sakowin, also known as the Great Sioux Nation, and within miles of the Standing Rock Sioux Tribe's primary intake for drinking water, without proper consultation or free, prior and informed consent. Since day one, we have been standing up against this blatant act of environmental racism and social injustice towards Indigenous Peoples.

The Standing Rock Sioux Tribe's water supply is officially at risk with the pipeline being fully operational. Many other Native and non-Native allies will continue to stand with Standing Rock and continue to organize to ensure Energy Transfer Partners is held accountable for the human rights crimes they have commit-ted, not just against Standing Rock but the many other Native nations along its path.

Statement from Standing Rock Sioux chairman Dave Archambault II:

Now that the Dakota Access Pipeline is fully operational, we find it more urgent than ever that the courts and administra-tion address the risks posed to the drinking water of millions of American citizens.

This pipeline became operational today, yet it has already leaked at least 3 times. This is foreboding as the company does not yet have a plan in place to address how they would contain and clean a serious spill.

We will continue to battle the operation of this pipeline in court and remind everyone that just because the oil is flowing now doesn't mean that it can't be stopped. The courts can stop it by demanding that the administration be held accountable for the full Environmental Impact Statement it initiated and then abandoned.

337. 350.org reported and commented, January 25, 2017.

338. Lauren Gambino, "Native Americans Take Dakota Access Pipeline Protest to Washington," *Guardian*, March 10, 2017, www.theguardian.com/us-news/2017/mar/10/native-nations-march-washington-dakota-access-pipeline.

339. Earth Justice report, June 14, 2017 (webpage no longer exists). More details and ongoing reports of the case, as of August 15, 2015, were available at Jan Hasselman, "On the Standing Rock Sioux Tribe Litigation: DAPL Ruling; What Was Decided, What's Next?" *Earth Justice*, June 15, 2017, http://earthjustice.org/features/dapl-ruling-what-was-decided-what-s-next.

340. Joseph Bullington, "From the Ashes of Standing Rock," *In These Times*, September 2017. On the Pilgrim Pipeline, "Overview," Coalition Against Pilgrim Pipeline (CAPP), https://stoppilgrimpipeline.com/. On the Tacoma, Washington, anti-natural gas plant effort, "Tacoma, WA Protesters Target Liquefied Natural Gas Plant," *Democracy Now!*, June 30, 2017, www.democracynow.org/2017/6/30/headlines/tacoma_wa_protesters_target_liquefied_natural_gas_plant.

341. Call to action by 350.org on August 16, 2017, https://act.350.org/donate/donate_idlenomore/?akid=24290.51426.5-v37R&rd=1&t=3&utm_medium=email&utm_source=actionkit (unfortunately this webpage no longer works). The entire statement read:

Indigenous activists from Idle No More San Francisco (SF) have been working with 350.org to stand up to Big Oil for years.

These brave warriors live near 5 oil refineries in what is known as the "refinery corridor." This corridor includes California's largest refinery, owned by Chevron. A 2012 explosion put this refinery on the map, sending 15,000 people to the hospital with respiratory problems.

In response, Idle No More SF organized 16 "healing walks" over the last four years. Watch this 5 min video to learn more [https://act.350.org/donate/donate_idlenomore/?akid=24290.51426.5-v37R&rd=1&t=3&utm_medium=email&utm_source=actionkit]:

These healing walks have brought to life a beautiful vision of different communities coming together to pray for clean air, clean water, and clean soil for all who live alongside these refineries.

Many of the communities near the refineries are people of color, poor people, and Indigenous Peoples. These communities experience high rates of respiratory problems, cancer and other health conditions due to the extreme air pollution the refineries create.[1]

Watch this short documentary, learn more about their work, and chip in.

350.org has proudly partnered with Idle No More SF in organizing and supporting past healing walks. In the months ahead Idle No More SF will be joining with 350.org and other partner organizations to begin work to stop new tar sands fossil fuel infrastructure projects.

Together, we are also organizing to make sure that California Governor Brown's 2018 Climate Summit lives up to its promises to communities in the refinery corridor.

Thank you for supporting Idle No More SF and 350.org's ongoing work to shut down these refineries and keep fossil fuels in the ground in the name of public health and a safe climate for all.

With deep gratitude,

Natalia

342. See, "Tell Banks: Do Not Fund the Trans Mountain Pipeline," CREDO Action, August 6, 2018, https://act.credoaction.com/sign/transmountain?t=2&akid=24400%2E1313914%2Esys5n.

343. "GLOBAL CLIMATE STRIKE → SEP. 20–27," https://globalclimatestrike.net, accessed October 8, 2019, stated,

---

1 Pollution, Poverty, People of Color: The factory on the hill.

20-27 September 2019, we saw a record 7.6 million people take to the streets and strike for climate action. The biggest climate mobilisation in history. From Jakarta to New York, Karachi to Amman, Berlin to Kampala, Istanbul to Québec, Guadalajara to Asunción, in big cities and small villages, millions of people joined hands and raised their voices in defense of the climate. The Global Climate Strike shows that we have the people power we need to create a just world and end the era of fossil fuels.

The website contains links to numerous media, including Somini Sengupta, "Protesting Climate Change, Young People Take to Streets in a Global Strike: Hundreds of thousands of young people around the world took to the streets on Friday to protest government inaction on the climate crisis," *New York Times*, September 21, 2019, www.nytimes.com/2019/09/20/climate/global-climate-strike.html.

See also: Eoin Higgins, "With Over 6 Million People Worldwide, Climate Strikes Largest Coordinated Global Uprising Since Iraq War Protests, The momentum is on our side and we are not going anywhere," *Common Dreams*, September 27, 2019, www.commondreams.org/news/2019/09/27/over-6-million-people-worldwide-climate-strikes-largest-coordinated-global-uprising?cd-origin=rss&utm_term=AO&utm_campaign=Daily%20Newsletter&utm_content=email&utm_source=Daily%20Newsletter&utm_medium=Email.

344. The topic of young Native activists in the environmental movement was discussed on *Native American Calling*, October 8, 2019: Art Hughes, "Tuesday, October 8, 2019—Young activists speaking for the environment," *Native America Calling*, October 8, 2019, www.nativeamericacalling.com:

Sixteen-year-old Swedish environmental activist Greta Thunberg's notoriety recently scolded world leaders over inaction on climate change at the UN General Assembly. Autumn Peltier (Anishinaabe) is a young First Nations environmental activist who also recently used the UN platform to speak up about the lack of clean water for Indigenous people in Canada. Xiuhtezcatl

Tonatiuh Martinez is part of a group of young people suing the US Government over climate change. Young Indigenous people are finding their voice and risking backlash, speaking up over climate change. Is their message being heard?

Guests:

Yang (Diné)—student at New Mexico School for the Arts as a visual artist, part of the steering committee for Youth United for Climate Crisis Action (www.youthunited4climatecrisisaction.org) (YUCCA),

Kimberly Pikok Piquk (Inupiaq)—student at the University of Alaska Fairbanks,

Bernadette Demientieff (Gwichyaa Gwich'in)—executive director of the Gwich'in Steering Committee (http://ourarcti-crefuge.org).

The Gwich'in Steering Committee website included the following in "The Gwich'in Steering Committee is Implementing a Youth Board," April 10, 2019, http://ourarcticrefuge.org/the-gwichin-steering-committee-is-implementing-a-youth-board/:

The input from our youth is vital to their future, and to the way we approach this fight to defend the Arctic National Wildlife Refuge. The youth board will consist of four youth. We are hoping for two youth for the US side, and two youth from the Canadian side. So that our youth board will represent a unified voice from both sides of the border in defense of the Arctic National Wildlife Refuge and the Porcupine Caribou Herd.

The roles and responsibilities for the youth board will consist of:

- Travel with GSC
- Being able to speak publicly
- Take the Media training GSC provides
- Advocate to defend the Arctic National Wildlife Refuge
- Be professional

Please encourage the youth from your community ages 15–17. They will have the opportunity to be advocates for the Gwich'in Nation, and for your communities. The applicants will need to submit a letter of intent and one recommendation letter from their Tribe. The first event we want them to attend is the Arctic Indigenous Climate Summit in Fort Yukon, Alaska from June 10-14th, 2019. Please apply keeping these dates in mind.

If you have interested applicants please contact: Julia Fisher-Salmon, GSC Executive Assistant. (907) 458-8264 or jfisher-salmon@gmail.com.

Among the numerous other reports of Indigenous American Youth in leadership on environmental issues, an October 5, 2019, email from the Lakota People's Law Project stated,

I'm excited to share with you that my friend, Greta Thunberg, is joining me for three events over the next three days in Lakota Country. More on that in a minute, but first, let me introduce myself. I'm Tokata Iron Eyes, daughter of Chase Iron Eyes, whom you have heard from many times in the past.

My father's work on behalf of Native justice and environmental concerns is also my work. I will add that, as a young woman of color, I focus much of my energy on the issues of Missing and Murdered Indigenous Women and the climate crisis, as they are particularly close to my heart. I may be a high school junior, but I have already traveled the world and made many appearances to speak on these critical topics, including at January's Women's March in Washington, D.C.

The Lakota People's Law Project is at 547 South 7th Street, #149, Bismarck, ND 58504-5859, info@lakotalaw.org, https://www.lakota-law.org.

On Greta Thunberg and Climate Strike, see Umair Irfan, "Greta Thunberg is leading kids and adults from 150 countries in a massive Friday climate strike: The international protest comes ahead of the UN Climate Action Summit," Vox, September 20, 2019, https://www.vox.com/2019/9/17/20864740/greta-thunberg-youth-climate-strike-fridays-future.

345. Gary Snyder, *The Old Ways: Six Essays* (San Francisco, CA: City Lights, 1977), 59–60.

346. "Raymond F. Dasmann: A Life in Conservation Biology," UC Santa Cruz University Library, http://library.ucsc.edu/reg-hist/dasmann. The following comments about Dasmann appear:

"Ray Dasmann innovated the lucid, non-political, and universally applicable idea [of] ecodevelopment.... His impact on conservation thinking has been fundamental.... So many eminent persons are credited with inventing new wheels, only to find that their predecessors were the originals. Ray is surely one of those, way ahead, even sometimes too far ahead, of his time. He has thought deeply, but written clearly, about the fundamentals of our relationships with, and dependency on nature."
—G. Carleton Ray

Raymond F. Dasmann's life as a conservation biologist during a half-century embraced both groundbreaking fieldwork and the effort to delineate the concepts which are the intellectual scaffolding of modern ecology. His lifework was shaped by a passion for the natural world and the desire to solve the environmental problems which threaten the planet....

Dasmann published numerous scientific articles and books, including *The Last Horizon* (1963), *The Destruction of California* (1964), *Planet in Peril?* (1971), *The Conservation Alternative* (1973), and his classic textbook, *Environmental Conservation* (5th edition, 1984), all of which have had lasting influence in modern conservation thinking and policy-making. He was involved in many environmental organizations, including the Wildlife Society, World Conservation Union, Earth Island Institute, the Central California Coast Biosphere Reserve, the World Wildlife Fund. Raymond F. Dasmann's life as a conservation biologist during a half-century embraced both groundbreaking fieldwork and the effort to delineate the concepts which are the intellectual scaffolding of modern ecology. His lifework was shaped by a passion for the natural world and the desire to solve the environmental problems which threaten the planet.

347. Snyder, *The Old Ways*, 61.
348. Ibid., 63.
349. Commoner, *Closing Circle*, 299.
350. Harris, Sachs, and Morris, *Re-Creating the Circle*, chap. 2.

Index to Volume II